Communication:

Silent Noise-A Global Perspective

Communication:
Silent Noise-A Global Perspective

Anuradha Malshe

SERIALS PUBLICATIONS
NEW DELHI (INDIA)

First Published – 2009

ISBN: 978-81-8387-252-2

Published by

SERIALS PUBLICATIONS
4800/24, 1st Floor, Ansari Road
Darya Ganj, New Delhi-110002 (India)
Phone : 23245225. Fax : 91-11-23272135
E-mail: serials@satyam.net.in

CONTENTS

Section–II
Art and Literature

Section–III
Reel and Ethereal

Section–IV
Law and Governance

Section–V
Business and Communication

THE RATIONALE

In February 2006, I had organized, coordinated and co-hosted an International Conference on "Communication" in conjunction with Sir JJ School of Art, Mumbai. Good friend Prof. John Steele (South Africa), who is a ceramist, was the chief guest. Art and communication was the central theme for deliberations that time. However this was not a one-off effort. It started a chain-reaction, a positive avalanche. For over two years I have constantly contemplated this concept, reformed, revised and fine-tuned it. What has evolved is amazing.

The conference was a starting point, the germ of an idea, which kick-started the idea of this book. Infact I have an extremely ambitious plan of doing a Trilogy about Communication. This book is the first one in the series. The second one, which I have already started working on, is about cinematic communication and the third and final one will be about, evolution of Language.

This book is about embracing dynamism in communication. This is a philosophy, which is born out of perception, multicultural understandings, gender-sensitive attitudes, inspired, broad-minded thinking and vivid imagination.

Communication has always been a fascinating concept which has been used and visualized in a multi-dimensional way. Print, electronic media, cinema, visual arts including performing arts, theatre even activism is communication. Anything that is a carrier of ideas, emotions, sentiments, concepts becomes communication. The expression of which may take diverse forms which are talked about. In fact when one takes a closer look, one can actually identify two distinct types: the message and the expression. Each one follows its own pattern and its own manifestation, but joins seamlessly to form a new entity or concept. Effective communication is the one which is successful in putting across the message without jeopardizing the expression or vice-versa. This is one pair scissors which cuts both ways.

The entire concept of this kind of eclectic collection is a wholly novel way of communication and so, consequently it explores equally novel, unconventional ideas, viz., chaos and activism. In fact communication evolves out of chaos, just the way the world was born.

Every thought, idea and concept, expressed or unexpressed, is born out of chaos; sometimes even of the silent noise variety. Even the myth of creation states that: first there was the thought then came the word and finally expression (begging thousand pardons of the real creator of this statement). For the uninitiated there is utter chaos of the mono-color variety. But once it is finely analyzed then one identifies, distinguishes and applauds chaos for its east-man color like qualities. The gifted ones contribute, while the non-gifted ones are the lookers-on. Every chaos takes a definite shape and is manifested as the "Expression". The thought is the "Message". These two things are the communication. Unless there is chaos, there can not be communication.

Activism is most certainly communication. Mutiny, friction, competition, revolution are all part of communication. Out of this communication, political activism and social activism is born. Quality, type, pattern and frequency of communication, writes the destiny of activism; either its long-lived success or early death. Many are the activist movements that have been still born, plainly because of lack of communication.

Cultural renaissance of Europe, the French and the Russian Revolutions, even the Industrial Revolution are all excellent case studies of successful communication.

This book is an amazing compilation of treatises, each distinct in its uniqueness and expression. The spectrum is wide and broad, ranging from mundane to ethereal. There is cinema, business, art, literature, intercultural- dimensions, technology and spirituality. Each discourse deals with a particular theme. The book is sub-divided into several sections. Each section deals with particular thematic concepts. I dare not divulge anything about the articles but would prefer to leave you to explore. By way of sneak preview, I would merely say that it is a cerebral treat, which I promise is extremely enjoyable. So happy reading!!!

Anuradha Malshe
January, 2009, India

LIST OF CONTRIBUTORS

Mr. Abhishek Chaudhary, *India,* has a graduation and post graduation in Management. He is a free lance film journalist, who writes fiction and non-fiction. He has presented papers at international conferences. Recently he has been to the Cannes International Film Festival. He has been closely associated with post-production movie launch of a new genre cinema. Presently he is working with a premier Production House.

Mr. Andika Putra Prathama, *Indonesia,* is pursuing 'Master of Science in Management' from Institut Teknologi Bandung, Indonesia. He has visited several countries like Austria, Finland, France, Italy, the Netherlands, and Switzerland. Besides management he has done courses related to intercultural communication like, Evolution of Language at Utrecht University, Utrecht, the Netherlands. Presently he is busy in organizing Bandung International Summer School in Astronomy.

Dr. Anuradha Malshe, *India,* completed her post graduation and doctorate from Mumbai University's economics department. Her doctoral work has been in the area of development banking. She has successfully completed projects for EXIM Bank, SICOM & ICICI. She has also worked on Education and has been part of the team on UN and Planning Commission assisted projects. Besides her doctorate, Anuradha also has post doctoral Research experience. Anuradha worked at the Fort Hare University, South Africa. She has also done NGO work in gender issues and community development. Anuradha has written several articles and research papers which have been published in India and abroad. She has already published books, on education of women and even on Bollywood. Currently her research interests are Gender issues, Inclusion Studies and Development Economics.

Mr. Felix Hofman, *Germany,* is a student of Political Science and has a degree in Political Science and Governance from the University of Passau, Germany. He has traveled extensively in North America, Polynesia, New Zealand and South-East Asia. Besides working abroad he has done a stint at the deanship of Naila, Germany. He is very active in the Model United Nations programme and visited several countries as a delegate. He is a professional pianist. Felix knows German, French, Spanish, English and Latin and has also been teaching the languages besides teaching music (piano). Presently, Felix is working with the Department for International Relations of the German Parliament, Berlin.

Mr. Govind Dhaske, *India,* has done Masters in Social Work from Tata Institute of Social Sciences, Mumbai. He holds in-depth experience on Non Profit Sector on rural development and health issues. Cultural innovations, social communications and folk art form based development communication strategies have been his research priority. He is a resource person and trainer for non-profit social organizations and has helped and advised found similar institutions. Govind writes extensively for national and international journals and has presented numerous papers. His research interests are Gender issues, Education Policy, Rural Development and Inclusion.

Ms. Mala Mody, *India,* is a proprietress of an Event management firm. She has successfully handled a variety of events ranging from film award functions to marketing events for adventure sports. She has also co-ordinated exhibitions of wares for home-based entrepreneurs, who otherwise do not have a platform.

Ms. Maria Juul Johanssen, *Denmark,* has received training as an Educator for teaching children with special needs. She has worked with children in primary school and with children with special needs. She has travelled extensively and has visited Sweden, Norway, Poland, Germany, France, Italy, Greece, Tenerife, Canaries, Egypt, the Netherlands, Spain, Finland and India. Currently she is pursuing an advanced degree, a Masters in Educational Sociology at the Danish School of Education, University of Aarhus, Denmark. Parallel with finishing the last year of her studies, she is working part-time in a consulting bureau.

Mr. Martin Weber, *Belgium* is a law student. He was a junior research assistant at the University of Passau, Germany. At the same university, he taught a tutorial on criminal law. He is also a freelance journalist and film critique. He writes about cultural events for local newspapers. Currently Martin is studying law at the Katholieke Universiteit Leuven, Belgium, where he assists a professor of law.

Prof. Mohandas Nair, *India* is an educator and consultant. He is from IIT (Kharagpur). He is into training and soft-skills. He holds workshops for industry personnel and also teaches and guides management students. He is Adjunct Professor teaching Soft Skills at IBS Mumbai. He has authored books and writes articles and research papers for national as well as international journals.

Ms. Karina Louise Peterson, *Denmark,* teaches Danish as a second language to adult students at the Copenhagen Intensive Language School. She has a Teacher's Education degree in Sociology and Education from Danish University of Education and has completed Teacher Practice training in Spain. Her special interests are Education systems and international assessments in educational politics.

Mr. Pantelis Bellis, *Greece,* has done his Masters in Education and Pedagogie from the University of Education in Western Macedonia, Greece. He received the prestigious Erasmus Scholarship and also studied at the University of Education Freiburg in Germany. Besides education Pete is also interested in intercultural studies and is at present pursuing his second Masters Cultural Studies in use of new Technologies in Education. Pete is a professional DJ and has over hundred fifty acts and appearances in Greece and other European countries. He also has over 24 official releases in different electronic music Labels around the World. He is into Image Processing and Website Developing Applications, Photography and Short Movie Productions. His research interests are Media, Culture, Communication and Education.

Prof. Prema Ramachandran, *Prema,* has a master's degree in English Literature and an MBA in HR from Viswabaharathi University. She has been teaching communication skills to engineering and MBA students for over a decade. Besides teaching writes extensively. Her areas of interest are muticultural communication and presentation skills. She is currently working on her doctorate. Presently she is editing a book on Shakespeare, which is an inter-disciplinary effort. Her research interests are visual art forms which represent the diverse Indian culture.

Mr. Rana Sinha, *Finland,* is a cross-cultural trainer and author. He was born in India, studied and lived in many places and traveled in over 80 countries, acquiring cross-cultural knowledge and building an extensive network of professionals. He has spent many years developing and delivering Cross-cultural Training, Professional Communications skills, Personal Development and Management solutions to different types of organizations and businesses in many countries. He now lives in Helsinki, Finland and runs http://www.dot-connect.com- which specializes in human resource development as well as communication and management skills training with cross-cultural emphasis. He writes regularly for his cross-cultural blog *http://originalwavelength.blogspot.com*

Dr. Vikram Nabar, *India,* holds a PhD in Engineering Sciences from the University of Cambridge (UK), where his work led to an understanding of the interactions between the aerodynamic and mechanical forces that normally cause failure of Turbomachinery Blades. Dr Nabar's industrial experience includes international assignments with companies such as the Central Electricity Authority (UK) and secondment as Technical Manager by Atlas Copco Ltd (Belgium) to its Air Compressor Manufacturing Project in Smederevo (Serbia). With an industrial (managerial and research) experience spanning over three decades, Dr. Nabar made an entry into the teaching profession in Feb. 1998 as the Head of the Department of Industrial and Production Engineering at the Vishwakarma Institute of Technology, Pune, India. At present he is Adjunct Professor of Operations Management & Organizational Behavior at ICFAI Business School, Pune, and is researching in multidisciplinary communications.

Section–I

Intercultural Communication

1

MY INTERCULTURAL GLASSES: INTERCULTURAL COMMUNICATION FROM AN INDONESIAN'S PERSPECTIVE

Andika Putra Pratama, Indonesia

"Having been travelling and meeting people from all over the world as well as getting intensively in touch with them in a relatively short time has been a very pleasant opportunity to initially feel and define what culture is. Personally, it is indescribable yet something that you can concretely feel."– A Personal Note.

MY CULTURE, YOUR CULTURE, AND INTERCULTURAL COMMUNICATION: AN INTRODUCTION

If you look into several textbooks, you may find various definitions about culture, though we may agree about one thing. Culture is like a coin. On one side, it reveals the characteristic of culture as being something shared with other people. This may lead us into talking about stereotype and things that come along with it. We may have specific common judgments about our own community and the others'. Such judgments may be either true or false, depending on what perspective we are observing from. Can we really say that Asians are more traditional than Europeans? From one context, it may be true. It is, however, not very wise to address this particular attribute to every single Asian or European. Therefore, this is what makes the other side of the coin exist.

At the same time, our shared attributes are the ones that may elicit our *uniqueness*. This can be achieved to its peak as one interacts with other people within various cultural contexts; In other words, *intercultural interactions* may open up such *opportunities* for one to explore his uniqueness within. And interactions here may be interpreted as either quantitative or qualitative ones, as well as either direct–not mediated by any secondary medium such as television or computer–or indirect ones. The more intercultural interactions one encounters, the more *opportunities* one has in getting affected by each, contributing to the uniqueness that one may possess. 'Will one even consider these *emerging opportunities* the real opportunities?' is another question. This part of the coin is all about expanding the horizon of one self in his attempt to get acquainted with any possible cultural attributes he is faced with.

This idea may lead us into thinking about the emergence of 'My Culture' and 'Your Culture', as this writing suggests, as the consequence of intercultural interactions. We may live in a community with shared culture, but our interactions with the *outer world* make us have something more to offer. Both ('my culture' and 'your culture') are defined as a set of identities that each human being possesses as intercultural interactions occur.

When talking about interactions, communication becomes a pivotal aspect. In a world of unstoppable mobility where humans have the opportunity to interact with other people from other parts of the globe, communication among people can be very much challenging. Thus, our uniqueness may somehow be subject to communication effectiveness; it is how we effectively communicate with others, how others can understand what we are trying to convey, through the best possible means. It is something that we have to practice almost every day and even every minute of a day.

My culture can even be very different from that of my father, mother and my close friends or a cumulative of my interactions with them. Culture as one of the properties that each human possesses really is something unique because one experiences many different paths and patterns of interaction with others. Nevertheless, it can be suggested that one have major contributors to his or her overall culture. Logically, when one spends more time with one particular community than with others, it is likely that he or she has some kinds of 'similar and shared' culture with the members of this community instead of with the others. But, when we talk about culture of a person, we also talk about intensity, how intense one person interacts with other people.

Consider a person who lives with other people for one or two weeks! He or she, for example, sees these people everyday and talks about several issues – sometimes personal ones – with them as well as learns about what they usually do; and these are done *intensely*. Do you ever watch such television shows as 'Worlds Apart,' in which modern American families have to live for a short period of time in some isolated areas in some other parts of the world, giving up their lifestyles and 'culture' that they use to carry with them and immersing themselves with the local customs, which are totally different from their owns.

At the end of the show, the members of the family usually have a kind of *life-changing experience* and confess that they are never going to be *the same again* after the experience. Here, we are talking about intensity. For these families, they can never escape from the fact that they have agreed to comply with the local customs, even when they do not *really* agree in the customs.

In this situation, communication may mean something more than just exploding words. It also means reconciliation with the unusual customs and strangers. It is the willingness of one person to get deeper into some spaces which can be vague at the beginning. But it does not mean giving up a whole belief system that one has been carrying. It is an attempt to refresh and reset just about anything that one possesses into one other structured belief, whatever it may be. It can be complementary or even total alteration for such a person. It is the moment of forming a kind of new 'shared culture' among very unlikely partners, a path towards *total understanding*.

BEING AN INDONESIAN

Although the national language of Indonesia is Indonesian (*Bahasa Indonesia*), or some just call it '*Bahasa*' (meaning simply 'language'), the fact that there are many different languages used in Indonesia tells that not everybody in this country speaks using the same language with each other every day. Indonesian people are considered bilingual in nature. It is very common that one has more than one mother tongue. One specific region has its own local language. What happens is more than just dialect differences.

These local languages are related to the fact that Indonesia has many ethnicities. On Java Island, for example, Javanese and Sundanese people are the major inhabitants. On this island, both Javanese and Sundanese languages are widely spoken and become the first languages of such regions. Even though these languages have roots in the same language, people from each ethnicity cannot simply speak with one another using their *own* language. Indonesian language is then preferred. It is indeed a normative version of Malay language, an Austronesian language that is also the mother for both Javanese and Sundanese languages.

Moreover, people from other parts of Indonesia (Sumatra, Kalimantan, Sulawesi, etc.) come to the island of Java to seek for better life and job, making this island the most populous in the world. This even adds to the exhortation that Indonesian has to be spoken as the national language. Nevertheless, there are some ethnics or sub-ethnics in some isolated areas that do not even know or can barely speak Indonesian language, the fact that makes people who want to come to such a place, for example, to do research find difficulties in communicating with them. For example, Baduy people only speaks some sub-division of Sundanese language, a kind of language that even common Sundanese people are not used to it in everyday life.

Their language is considered profoundly coarse or a low-leveled Sundanese. Their inability in speaking Indonesian may be due to their restriction or limitation of having such contact with outsiders.

One extreme case may happen when two people speaking to each other using two different languages; one speaks using Indonesian and one using another. Funnily, they engage in a relatively productive conversation. This happens usually when both have the same ethnicity. For example, one has both Indonesian and Sundanese as his or her mother tongues but is more used to only one of these languages in daily conversation. In some other cases, one uses a mix of these languages. People in the border of West Java and Central Java may speak a language that is a Sundanese-Javanese mix, creating new dialects different from both ethnics.

Adding to dialects, communication tone is also an important factor when one communicates with one another, coming from different cultural backgrounds. For example, Batak people somehow need to adjust their tone when speaking to Sundanese people in, of course, Indonesian language. It is the nature of Sundanese people that they are more likely to speak in a low-intonated manner, which is quite the opposite of what Batak people naturally do. It is very likely that misunderstanding and misinterpretation happen during such conversation. Thus, one simple thing that one has to do is to reconcile with it and moreover, make fun of the people without even attempting to degrade them or the language. It is solely for the purpose of creating such a (cultural) bond.

What makes Java Island especially pivotal is that it serves as a medium of cultural learning for both the original islanders and (especially) outsiders. It is the place for achieving reconciliation of culture due to the broad range of cultures on the island and everyday interaction.

INDONESIA AND INVASION OF FOREIGN LANGUAGES

Adding to the fact mentioned previously that Indonesian people are bilingual in nature, the invasion of English language is inevitably happening in some parts of Indonesia, making communication seem to be more challenging. This is happening especially in such major cities as Jakarta and Bandung. For some, English has gained its status as one language to use in daily basis, realizing the fact that English has become the international language for everyone to master. It is especially important for those who are expecting international encounters.

Being used to mixing Indonesian and other local languages, Indonesian people are now prone to mixing English with Indonesian. It often happens in academic life. English terms often collide with Indonesian expressions. The whole language mixing thing is inevitable for some Indonesians. They cannot escape from the fact that they find better words in one of these languages to express what they want to convey. Most of the time, all of this happens in an informal context, where one is more comfortable with one language than another. However, it can also happen in such formal contexts as meeting and class presentation.

The use of English in daily basis is also urged by the emerging (partial or full) English-medium institutions, which include universities, international (primary and secondary) schools and Islamic schools (called '*Pesantren*' in Indonesian). It is at the moment one of the hottest issues faced by post-secondary educations. Unfortunately, universities do not explicitly provide the 'real' language course to both the students and faculties. They still maintain admission to prospective students who *only* have TOEFL score of 475 to 500, which is still considered low for universities which want to adopt English as the medium of instruction. Even when they are admitted, there has been no real support to improve their competency during their study. For faculties, those who are used to English are usually those who have completed their studies in an English-medium university abroad. Inevitably, they also bring some portions of the culture of one particular university abroad–and moreover, the country itself–to the university in which they teach. As a result, communication among academia can be very much complex, in terms of the language used and how one perceives the use of such language.

Islamic schools have different stories. They usually implement three languages in their schools: English, Indonesian and Arabic. The use of these languages is mandatory; one language for one day or more. They learn Arabic because it is the language of the Islamic holy book, *Al-Qur'an* (Koran, in English). So, the demand is higher in Islamic schools as they are obliged to master both English and Arabic. This is undeniably good for them when they want to continue their study further to higher education, for example, in the Middle East where Arabic is widely spoken. More importantly, when you can speak either English or Arabic, it is easier for you to approach international audience for religious awareness purposes.

If Arabic is mandatory in Islamic schools, such foreign languages as German, French and Japan are made obligatory in such secondary schools. So at least, some Indonesian youngsters are capable of saying some basic words in one of these languages. It is probably an attempt to be prepared for the expansion of other non-English speaking countries that enact the importance of learning their language.

FUTURE COMMUNICATION FOR INDONESIANS

Only few facts are known by the world about Indonesia. Despite being the 16th largest country in the world, not so many people can tell about its location. It seems that world inhabitants know Bali more than Indonesia itself, even though it is just one considered tiny island being a part of Indonesia. Even Indonesian people themselves are likely to have little knowledge about their country, specifically, some other areas away from their own province and island. It is because Indonesia is a very plural country. Extremely said, there is no such thing as the culture of Indonesia.

"Visit Indonesia 2008," a tourism program initiated by the Indonesia's Ministry of Tourism and Culture, may seem to people as an attempt to introduce the whole Indonesia and, at the same time, one specific region in Indonesia to its own people and the world, hoping that Indonesian people are willing to come to other regions and people from abroad will be willing to explore and experience Indonesia and its regions. Each province has its own way of marketing themselves. It is indeed true because more and more international tourists are coming to Indonesia nowadays, adding to the intercultural experience that an Indonesian could have.

The challenge in communication for Indonesians is therefore getting bigger as international inhabitants are *moving*–really moving–towards Indonesia, the once-unknown country. Language difference will be a barrier somehow if Indonesian people refuse to be immersed with aliens. It is inevitably crucial for all Indonesians to be able to speak English fluently, nowadays. Nobody is supposed to impose your language on foreigners. We shall not forget the philosophy behind language: *communication promoting understanding.*

Challenges in communication are very obvious for Indonesians. First of all, nobody really speaks Indonesian, except Indonesian people themselves. *For the local languages?* The case is somewhat the same. Secondly, English has replaced Indonesian language in several daily conversations, especially in academic and working contexts. Thirdly, other foreign languages have been compulsory subjects for high school students. It can somehow be predicted that these languages, such as German, may also gain the same status as what English has achieved now.

In the national context, everywhere in Indonesia, you can find such advertisement saying–more or less–that "use Indonesian for daily conversation." It can be seen as an attempt to make Indonesians aware of their own national language as a part of their identity. So, for example, when people come from the eastern to western part of Indonesia, they will find it easy to communicate with the local people and easily feel welcomed due to the 'shared' language they speak. However, it can also be seen as a threat for the local people and their languages.

The importance of English in Indonesian people's daily basis seems to be somewhat a threat for the use of Indonesian language as the national language. In what sense should it be a threat? *Let's face it!* The fact is that Indonesian is the country's national language (which for some cases, the second language of Indonesian people) and English is the commonly-believed international language. It implies that every Indonesian has to speak Indonesian language with other Indonesians and English with foreign people. Nevertheless, a lot of Indonesians, especially those living in big cities, prefer to speak English with other Indonesians as well just to prepare themselves for international encounters. So, what will the future hold? It is a question that depends a lot on how we see all of this, as Indonesian, English, the local languages and other foreign languages are spoken widely.

MY INTERCULTURAL EXPERIENCES AND COMMUNICATION: A PERSONAL NOTE

This chapter is dedicated to personal experiences of being in such short-term intercultural activities involving a broad range of people from various places around the world. Having been travelling and meeting people from all over the world as well as getting intensively in touch with them in a relatively short time has been a very pleasant opportunity to initially feel and define what culture is. Personally, it is indescribable yet something that you can concretely feel.

It started in 2006 when I was still a final-year student of Astronomy Department at *Institut Teknologi Bandung* (ITB, Bandung Institute of Technology), in Bandung, Indonesia. Prior to this year, my intercultural experiences were still limited to the ones involving such ethnicities in Indonesia.

First of all, ITB is quite a multicultural university. Students from all over the country study at ITB, one of the best universities in Indonesia. In other words, we have students from various ethnicities; they not only come from Java Island in which Sundanese and Javanese people are the major inhabitants, but also Sumatra, Kalimantan, Bali, Sulawesi, Papua and even from smaller islands, that undeniably could bring their own 'shared' culture to Bandung and, at the same time, try to settle and accustom themselves to the local customs (i.e. Sundanese customs). Some are willing to even learn about the local language (Sundanese), even though a lot of people in the region speak Indonesian. It is especially advantageous when they talk to local sellers (vendors) who usually settle along the sidewalk of every street and every corner of the street. We usually call these people 'Pedagang Kaki Lima'. And even some sellers coming from other regions of Indonesia speak Sundanese in order to create such a friendly environment.

It was March-April 2006 that I was introduced to the fact that there is such thing called 'summer school'. I was somehow excited, but nothing really motivated me to apply. The summer school was called 'Utrecht Summer School in Astrophysics (USAP) 2006.' In short, I eventually applied due to the very unlikely meeting with my friend who managed to encourage me. Then I, along with three of my friends, was admitted to the summer school, with scholarship in hand. In short (again), we were in Utrecht, the Netherlands. I was really happy because I could finally practice my English, which was my actual goal. So, I met new friends here; they are from Greece, Spain, Turkey (who were my roommates), the United States, Estonia, Italy, Portugal and Belarus.

In our first evening (my roommates and I), the first thing we were talking about was frankly religion. Everybody introduced their own religion and their connection with it. The idea was that I had the opportunity to introduce my belief and faith (Islam). We had very great yet tough discussions in some evenings during the two-week summer school. I finally realized that it would take me to some other miles to be able to convey to them what I really wanted and needed to convey. These were the first time ever for me to face such challenge. I could not escape from this discomfort that I could not perfectly deliver my thoughts to them. It was my first time also to encounter such a situation where everybody would just say what he *really* wanted, while at the same time, we remained friends. I could completely sense the intercultural interaction and communication to a whole new level.

In my country, it is very usual for Muslims, Christians and other religions to sit side by side and appreciate what each has to practice. I knew that it was going to be different in Europe in general, especially after the 9/11 tragedy and other terrorist activities involving (*so-called* Muslim) fanatics. Basically, Muslims have to pray five times a day. Indonesian Christians, for example, are accustomed to the way Muslims practice their (our) religion. Here in the Netherlands, I realized that it was going to be a different story for all of us.

A year after (2007)–because of the infectious environment that I was involved in–I was doing it over again, another summer school in Utrecht, the Netherlands. But this time, I already graduated and took 'the Evolution of Language' as the course in the summer school, which was just a reason for me to escape for the routines back in Indonesia and try to experience some other possible interested things away from home. In this year, the summer school was only for a week but I decided to travel around to France, Switzerland, Austria and Germany before the actual summer school. Intercultural communication was still something to talk about.

In the same year, (December 2007), I decided to apply for an intercultural activity called 'Social Enterprise for Economic Development,' a collaboration between the School of Business and Management (SBM-ITB) and the Asia Research Center of the University of St. Gallen, which took place in Bandung and Cisondari Village in Indonesia. The other participants are from Switzerland, Singapore and Germany. At the time, I was still in my first semester of my Master's Program in *Science in Management* at SBM-ITB with the whole hectic schedule I was having. I gave up my study for two weeks just to be involved again in an intercultural environment. Interestingly, religion (Islam) became one of the topics to address as well. But this time, it was not really a discussion. It was more about witnessing how we (Muslims) practice our religion. Along with witnessing, questions were also raised.

The following year, I could not help myself to apply for another summer school. This year's course that I took was called 'Developing Intercultural Competence' (which was really perfect for what I have been into) in Helsinki, Finland. Again, it took me to another level. The name of the course said it all. I had the chance to practice my intercultural sensitivity, using observation and communication styles. It was about how you communicate with other people from different cultures and how to overcome such obstacles. Moreover, you could really feel the essence of culture. Everybody became an ambassador of their own *origin*.

FINISHING TOUCH...

In conclusion, (intercultural) communication seems to be more than just communication through words. It is about how you allow people to get acquainted with your culture (identity) and how you allow yourself to be introduced to another culture, which does not state that you have to believe in *that* culture. It is more than just exploding words as the first chapter suggests. It is about reconciliation with the unusual customs and strangers. Communication is not about imposing your thoughts and beliefs. It is about bridging these thoughts and beliefs with others', which (once again) does not suggest that you have to comply with their thoughts and beliefs.

Being an Indonesian has been a very nice opportunity to firstly get to know what it means by intercultural communication. Moreover, our involvement in the world and the invasion of foreign languages seem to be a trigger for Indonesians to reconcile with any possible encounters. Our (Indonesians') position is in ideal place to expand, seek for, and get acquainted with (better) intercultural media.

This article has been about my intercultural glasses on (intercultural) communication, about what has been established and what the future may hold in relation to current states, from an Indonesian's perspective. It has been a personal note and a reservoir for my intercultural experiences. As this writing suggests, intercultural communication has to be practiced every day and even every second of a day. The outcome would be something beyond our imagination, just like *the initiation and realization of this writing*: a true outcome of effective intercultural communication.

2

"DEVELOPING INTERCULTURAL COMPETENCE" AS A PEDAGOGICAL ACT– THE HELSINKI SUMMER SCHOOL 2008 CASE

Pantelis Bellis, Greece

INTRODUCTION

In a complex and constantly changing world, where processes like Globalization and marginalization of Cultures take part, it seems important for the Individual to develop skills, competences and attitudes, which help him look forward to a brighter and every day better future (Trilianos, 1997/98; Matsagouras, 1998). Thus, in a meta-modern context, where the process of perceiving, decoding and sending messages depends both on individual as well as on cultural factors (Bluedorn, 1998), it is essential for the individual to develop communicational and interpretational skills. The mutual understanding and respecting of the "other" on communicational situations, as well as the creative approach of cultural differences, create in that way, a context where the importance of communication lies on the process of reflection and self reflection of the individual (Bennet, 1993; Tanno, 2000). Therefore, a worldwide debate appears, referring to the importance of Educational and Pedagogical processes – acts, and presenting them as a constant trade of information between the participants. Lipman (2003), seems to emphasize on that too, by supporting Dewey who presents the educator's role in such processes, more as intermediary than dominant. The declining instructive course of the educator, and consequently, the transformation of dual Pedagogic relation in that of a team, is considered as an integral piece of such an approach, that requires the self-activity of the participants, but also the communication and collaboration between them (Matsagouras, 2000; Kapsalis, 2002). That way, in any educational situation, a community of Inquiry (Lipman, 2003) is created, in which communication and discussion through working in Groups, provide a suitable background for the negotiation of meanings and perceptions, the examination of causes and choices, and the evaluation of interpretations (Lipman, 2003). By participating in this process the participants can evaluate their arguments (Lipman, 2003), extend the arguments of the general network (Lipman, 2003) and finally interact and dynamically develop their cognitive, critical and communicational skills (Ikuenobe, 2002). Of course, these processes demand the proper context referring to time, place, organization and the general structure of it.

An interpretation and evaluation of such a process will follow. It will be a reflection (on the theoretical and practical context) on the experiences of a student (educator and postgraduate student on Human Studies) of the Helsinki (Finnland) Summer School 2008, which where acquired in a period of three weeks, on the Course "Developing Intercultural Competence". Thus, the examination will refer to the Course as a Pedagogical Act (containing the "Methodology" of Science, "the approach and expression" of Arts and the "searching for answers about Humans' and not only Identity" of Philosophy) and examine it from an educators view. The examination will emphasize on the processes of communication and interaction (Group Work) and on the organizational and structural context of the Course, using two Paradigmatic Tasks (out of seven) and their theoretical background, which were written by the student for the Course.

OBSERVATION AND INTERPRETATION

First Paradigmatic Task

- Observe (during following days) different communication styles used. What communication styles people use? Who uses what, in what situation? How do you recognize the communication style? In other words: what are the characteristics of that communication style?
- Identify the communication styles you are using.
- Try communication style that you do not normally use. How was your experience; the others' reaction?

Communication, either Verbal or through body language, face expressions or behaviour, refers to the overall values and patterns of the participants on the communication cultures (Bennet, 1991). Depending on the amount of information which is provided, the context in which the communication takes part can be high or low (Bluedorn, 1998; Francesco, 1998). Still, communication in any context means a balance between "understanding, misunderstanding and lack of understanding". Thus, communication is based on the interpretation of the transmitted messages (either verbal or not), on mutual understanding and on language itself (Nynäs, 2006). The Observation and interpretation of such "Communicational situations", is a reflection on the experiences (in the theoretical and practical context) of a student of the Helsinki Summer School 2008, which were acquired in a period of two (2) weeks. Of course such an act is as objective as perceiving from an article that "Nacirema" ("American" backwards) Culture is far away from the American culture (Miner, 1956). Still, it will include an effort of an examination through the communication styles people use in different situations. A self reflection on using communication styles will follow together with a paradigmatic situation, where a different than the preferred communication style has been used. The communication styles which are going to be used refer most on Bennets' article "Verbal Communication Styles". Such styles are: Direct and indirect style, elaborate and succinct style, personal and contextual style, instrumental and affective style.

Direct Style: It was observed that it was mostly used on situations where clear and concrete information was needed such as low context situations, e.g., cashiers, on the tram or when asking a "local" for directions. Without many expressions (not more than a smile and a fast eye contact) and body language the information just "flew" from the one participant on the communication to the other. The style could be used either from people who have a personal relationship or not. Still it was observed mostly between strangers.

Indirect Style: Style which was mostly used on situations where the information–message should be transmitted more carefully "in order to avoid leaving an assertive impression" (Bennet, 1991). This communicational style was mostly observed to happen between people who have had a formal relationship. For example on "lecture situations" where the lecturer wanted to avoid a negative evaluation of a student's comment.

Elaborate Style: This style combined with a kind of affective style was observed to be used on situations, where the participants wanted to impress each other with a "rich and expressive language" or even on class situations where students wanted to express their thoughts with a rich and as much as possible high context language.

Succinct Style: The Succinct style was observed when communicating with Finnish and Asians. On uncertain and unpredictable social interactions (Bennet, 1991) with strangers mostly, they tend to use pauses and silence while the communicational act took part.

Personal Style: This style was used in situations where individuals wanted to set a context where power was distributed. It refers to "individual-centered language" (Bennet, 1991) where individuals wanted to present their "qualities". Mostly preserved on "Group work situations", where informality and symmetrical power distribution was perceived of them to be needed.

Contextual Style: This style referred to a "role-centered language" (Bennet, 1991). This style was often used in class situation from students coming from "hierarchical cultures" or "educational systems" in order to put themselves in "proper role positions and hierarchical status" in relation to the lecturer.

Instrumental Style: This style as "sender oriented", uses goal orientation. It is used from individuals who want to make themselves understandable by talking on a step to step conversation (Bennet, 1991). It was observed on "intellectual conversations" between participants who wanted to present their status and knowledge about specific subjects and not only. This style was mostly used by individuals who were using low context communicational styles.

Affective Style: This style was observed when individuals were using a receiver oriented language. In a high context communication, individuals who are using this style aim for a relational definition and approval (Bennet, 1991). It was observed on situations where participants tended to "sense" the content of a discussion more than to "logically" perceive it.

The communication styles which are preferred to be used by the student depend not only on his personal and cultural background but also on the context he communicates (referring to the place, the time and the participants on the discussion). Good communication means being able to decode messages and speak a common language in a content of respecting and mutual understanding of each others communicational needs (Nynäs, 2006). Still, through these two (2) weeks of self reflection in Helsinki, some essential parts of the students' communicational behavior could be observed. Such were:

The "use of Direct communication style with purpose to express thoughts, opinions and expectations without being afraid to make a mistake": Even though these competencies seem to be part of the characteristics of an intercultural effective person (Vulpe, 2000), it is noted, that this direct way of "free" expressing sometimes lacks on cultural sensitivity and therefore, it can lead to uncomfortable situations. Another essential part of the way of communication of the student is the "use of high context communicational behavior". By using rich body language, face expressions and verbal "variety" on the tone and the volume of the voice it is possible to attract the attention of the participants for the communicational process. Still, this way of communicating may, many times lacks flexibility and integration with situations where low context communication is needed. Heavy eye contact is used in any situation, sometimes body contact and "many times just interrupting in the discussion socially affective verbal communication style", by using superlatives and showing that way, more than enough, interest to different situations. Thus, it is easy to establish shared meanings with people, but also to disrespect their "private space" in communication and so make them feel uncomfortable.

The paradigm with the use of a totally different communication style than the usual one for the student, follows:

The place where the observation was held was a night club in Helsinki, and the time was a Friday evening and the participants were three girls and two boys. The student in question had just got introduced to two girls in the group and the third girl in the group he already knew. There were also two boys in the group. One was a good friend of the student and he also knew the other one, though not very well.

Trying to use a totally different communication style that he usually prefers to use, the student got in uncomfortable communicational situations. By trying to be as "silent as possible", by using the succinct style and by trying to respect as much as possible the different opinions of others, by using the indirect style, he managed to respect their "private communicational space" as much as possible by not interrupting them and not even using eye or body contact.

The Main Result of the Observation was that the four (4) of the 5 participants stopped communicating with the student. His "self-confinement", was interpreted and evaluated as rude and antisocial. Still, it was interesting to observe that, the two (2) Girls he got introduced that night and the boy he did not know very well, didn't give him many chances to communicate. On the other hand his friend and the one (1) of the three girls (the one whom he knew already) showed some kind of a respect to his behavior and didn't judge him. Still, it seemed that the stereotype of the enthusiastic and loud Greek (the student is a Greek person) using affective style, eye contact, body language and body contact would be the right one, even in the participants' eyes, in a loud and crowded place where people go to chat and have fun. The observation and its interpretation and evaluation show the importance of being "oneself", trying to play roles but still not adopt them and always considering the context where the communication and interaction take place. Here one needs to keep in mind, time, place and participants in the communication set-up.

PARADIGMATIC TASK: INTERCULTURAL GROUP DYNAMICS

Even though temporary group work on a multicultural context of cultural similarities but also diversities seems a priori to be seen as a difficult task, it can lead to a "creative" process, where new ideas and new perspectives are presented (Adler, 2002). The importance of the team refers to a variety of perspectives and solutions to a problem and helps the creation of a "network" between people (Schneider, 2002). Innovation, as a process of the development and the implementation of new ideas by people, who are engaged with others to an institutional context, is very important (Newell, 2000). Trust, as an expression of dealing with risks, vulnerability and uncertainty, could be another parameter which could affect the results of a group working together (Newell, 2000; Meyerson, 1996). Temporary groups have a short lifespan and form themselves around a goal and a purpose (Meyerson, 1996), therefore a context of cultural synergy is essential to them (Adler, 2002). That way, Cultural differences are seen as opportunities and the decisions and results of the team can accomplish high standards of quality (Schneider, 2002).

During the course "Developing Intercultural Competence", the Student could work in Groups, observe, interpret, evaluate and after all experience in various, different ways "in group situations".

The "group workshops" took place on three different occasions. A reflection and self reflection by the student on all this, by using the model of Schneiders' Article "Managing across cultures", is what follows:

Creating a sense of purpose (specific performance, goals and objectives): The Creation of a common sense of purpose within the group and the set of specific goals and objectives, was always essential to the results on any group work. Thus, a collective perception was created within the group for managing issues. The student always tried to contribute to the creation of such a context by using a combination of a direct and socially affective communication style.

Structuring the Task: As mentioned before, the contribution from the student, on the "creation of a sense of purpose", was in any case essential to the group work process. Therefore, the groups usually tended to give the student a centre role in organizing and structuring the tasks. Still, in order to keep the power distribution balanced, the student was always asking the group members on how "they could act together". He was always supportive in a positive way and ready to contribute to the discussion with a direct style.

Assigning roles and possibilities: "Huddling" (Gannon, 2003) seemed to be important to the assignment of roles and possibilities. The importance of time on being as much effective (meaning by that the end of the tasks) as possible, was in any group essential. It seemed that the common goal always was this kind of effective way of working. That way, a closer come together of the participants and a fast presentation of each one's preferences and competences to the others, could always lead to a "phenomenological" or at least, right assignment of roles in the group. That way a "competitive specialization" (Gannon, 2003) could occur, where the "right" (concerning every ones individual talents and interests) tasks, roles, possibilities and responsibilities could be assigned to anyone of the participants. This "celebration" of cultural and personal approaches, views and opinions could continue with the presentation of each one's work–results, in the group.

Reaching decisions: After presenting the results of the individual sub-tasks in the group, a discussion usually followed. Through the discussion, the individuals in the group could reflect and present to each other views and opinions. Usually the discussions took place in a context of mutual understanding and trust. In the discussions, the student, rather preferred to make compromises with his opinions and views, than to be insistent about something. The context was always respectful to other's opinions and the decisions were taken through a consensus. Still, in cases where the minority insisted to a decision, this decision was also a part of the groups' decisions.

Eliciting participation: Even though in any case, the groups seemed to work very good and "efficient", some factors (either cultural or personal) where observed to affect the "group processes". Most of them had to do with: Time–efficiency, power distribution and stereotypes within the group, (individual–collective) culture differences and gender similarities as well as differences. Concerning the time and efficiency, "there was never enough time" for people to express really what they thought. Not everyone uses direct communication style, or instrumental communication style so that he can be as concrete as possible in as less time as possible. Thus, for cultural and personal communicational reasons, some people where actually almost excluded from the context of the group work. Especially individuals from Asian countries with a collectivistic cultural background and many times high context communicational behaviors, were affected by that phenomena. Still, through the competitive specialization mentioned before, these individuals could have the chance to provide and present their work to the group. Power distribution and stereotypes between the group also sometimes led to misunderstandings. The one being always the "loudest" and not afraid to express his thoughts and feelings (even if they seemed a bit "irrational" sometimes) in the group and in the class, was preferred to organize and steer the group. That way someone who is used to be silent and take his time and space could be excluded. Finally, referring to gender differences, it was observed that sometimes problematic situations occurred between the male participants of the group in power distribution situations. These were easily treated though by making some compromises, either the one way or the other. Differences between men and women were treated most of the time with a nice smile and a gentle eye contact.

Importance of power in the group: The importance of power in the group is more or less described in the previous stages, while "power" always occurs and has an effect on human relations.

Evaluate and reflect: the sending and perceiving feedback in any case was an essential to the groups' work. It seemed that for negative evaluations the indirect communication style and silence were used. While in positive evaluations a direct affective style was used, combined sometimes even with humor and comments. It seemed that the participants tended to be much more communicative and expressive in positive evaluation situations than in negative ones.

In general the group work seemed to be very interesting and productive. While working together with people, on a safe multicultural context (referring to the time, the place the workshops took part, the way the teams were combined from the contractor and the general structure of the workshops (Meyerson, 1996)), the students could actually combine their powers, build on their similarities - differences and through an obligation, a contract of trust (Newell, 2000), they could put in question their negative stereotypes about the others and at the end "paint a new picture of them" (Illman, 2006).

EVALUATION AND DISCUSSION

The two Paradigmatic Tasks were presented as they are, with purpose to refer to processes which were essential for the course. The Intensive work, interaction and discussion (while working in groups together or in class situations), the use of methods of Observation, Interpretation and Evaluation and the combination of Theory and Practice on a constant process of Reflection and Self Reflection seemed to be the most important of them. All this, combined with the safe multicultural and "helpful" for the students' context[1], could lead to a Pedagogical understanding and not only Act and Process, which included discussion, communication, Group Work and Interaction, Observation, Interpretation and

Evaluation. It also had a way of "approaching" and "expressing" inner thoughts and feelings of Arts, the Methodological approach of Sciences and the quest for answers about human and not only nature, of Philosophy.

Using Bennets' Article "Towards Ethnorelativism: A Developmental Model of Intercultural Sensitivity", someone could conclude that Pedagogical acts and socialization processes take part from the beginning of any individuals' life. Through life experiences, education and interaction, someone can become a "better person". The definition of that refers on the social context someone lives. In that sense, being a better person refers more or les to "being socially integrated". Still, on a dynamic multicultural context, where pluralism is highly appreciated, there is a need for the individual to become as less as possible ego-centric and as much as possible relative on his way of acting, living, interacting and communicating. The "Developing Intercultural Competence" Course helped the student to adapt new communication skills and experience life from another point of view (empathy) and actually respect cultures as highly as oneself through a generalized world view (pluralism). Through different communicational processes, he could analyze and evaluate situations from different perspectives in specific contexts. He got more and more interested in the dynamic process of "being in-between cultures" and so he realized that not only knowing cultures and their structures, but also experiencing them on a dynamic process, can contribute to constructive marginality and personal growth.

NOTE

1. Refers to the well structured Summer School and allied activities as also the fascinating experience of staying and studying in the city of Helsinki which comes out as a multi-dimensional culture city full of choices and open possibilities.

REFERENCES

Adler, Nancy (2002), International Dimensions of Organizational Behaviour, Chapter 5: Creating Cultural Synergy.

Bennet, Milton J. (1991), Verbal Communication Styles. In: Culture and Interpersonal Communication.

Bennett, Milton J. (1993), Towards Ethnorelativism: A Developmental Model of Intercultural Sensitivity. In: Paige, Michael (Ed.) Education for the Intercultural Experience.

Bluedorn, A. C. (1998), An Interview with Anthropologist Edward T. Hall. In: *Journal of Management*, Inquiry 7, No. 2.

Francesco, A.M. and Gold, B. A. (1998), Frameworks for Examining Cultures. In: International Organizational Behaviour. Text, Readings, Cases, and Skills.

Gannon, Michael J. (2003) 3, Understanding Global Cultures: Metaphorical Journeys through 28 Nations, Clusters of Nations, and Continents, Sage Publications.

Ikuenobe P. (2002), Epistemic Foundation for Teaching Critical Thinking in Group Discussion. In: Interchange 33/4. Netherlands: Kluwer Academic Publishers.

Illman, Ruth (2006), Stereotypes: The Symbolic Image of the Other. In: Dahl, Jensen, Nynäs: Bridges of Understanding. Perspectives on Intercultural Communication. Oslo Academic Press.

Kapsalis, A. G. (2002) 3, Paidagogiki Psychologia. Athens: Kyriakidhs

Lipman M. (2003) 2, Thinking in Education. UK: Cambridge University

Matsagouras, I. (2000), Omadosynergatiki Didaskalia. Athens: Grigoris

Matsagouras, I. (1998), I kritiki skepsi sti didaktiki praksi: Diapistoseis, protaseis kai apotelesmata. In: Pedagogiki epitheorisi 27.

Meyerson, Debra, Weick Karl E. and Kramer, Roderick M. (1996), Swift Trust and Temporary Groups. In: Trust in Organizations.

Miner, Horace (1956), Body Ritual of the Nacirema. In: American Anthropologist Journal, 58. (Source text as PDF: *http://www.aaanet.org/pubs/bodyrit.pdf, at 7.08.2007).*

Nynäs, Peter (2006), Interpretative Models of Estrangement and Identification. In: Dahl, Jensen, Nynäs: Bridges of Understanding. Perspectives on Intercultural Communication. Oslo Academic Press.

Newell, S. and Swan, J. (2000), Trust and Inter-organizational Networking. In: Human Relations, 53(10), 1287-1327.

Schneider, Susan C. and Barsoux, Jean-Louis (2002), Managing Across Cultures, Chapter 8: The 'Multicultural' Team. Prentice Hall: Pearson Education.

Tanno, Dolores V. (2000), Names, Narratives, and the Evolution of Ethnic Identity. In: González, Houston, Chen: Our Voices. Essays in Culture, Ethnicity and Communication.

Trilianos, A. (1997/98), I Kaliergeia tis Kritikis skepsis sto sxolio. In: Makednon 4.

Vulpe, Thomas (2000), A Profile of the Interculturally Effective Person. Ottawa: Centre for Intercultural Learning, Canadian Foreign Service Institute.

3

COMMUNICATION AS THE BRIDGE BETWEEN YOU AND ME

Maria Juul Johanesson, Denmark

If One is truly to Succeed in Leading a Person to a Specific Place, One must First and Foremost Take Care to Find Him where He is and Begin There. This is the Secret in the Entire Art of Helping.

Anyone who cannot do this Himself is under a Delusion if He thinks he is able to Help Someone else. In order truly to help Someone else, I must Understand more than he–but certainly First and Foremost Understand what He understands.

If I do not do that, then my greater Understanding does not help Him at all. If I nevertheless want to assert my greater Understanding, then it is because I am Vain or Proud, then basically instead of benefiting Him I really want to be admired by Him. But all true Helping begins with a Humbling.

The Helper must First Humble Himself under the Person he wants to Help and thereby Understand that to Help is not to Dominate but to Serve, that to Help is a not to be the most Dominating but the most Patient, that to Help is a Willingness for the Time being to put up with being in the Wrong and not Understanding what the Other understands.

Kierkegaard, S. (1813-1855)

INTERCULTURAL COMPETENCE AND COMMUNICATION

During three weeks in August 2008 I participated in a course named "How to Develope Intercultural Competence" at the University of Helsinki. Our class represented a rich cultural variation with 24 students all from different countries. Even though our class was compounded of students or graduated students at a Bachelor/Master level, we developed and expanded our cultural competences, became consciousness of different communication strategies and experienced different encounters and interpretations.

The challenges of transforming the theoretical intercultural knowledge to practice showed for instance that as well as theories can be interpreted differently depending on the cultural glasses one use, this variety in understanding and interpretations influenced on how to determine the solution in a progressively and creatively way. The course emphazised the importance of making a promotion of developing intercultural competence, education and communication for everyone, who is living in a globalized society now and in the future.

Because of the globalization the world already seems smaller today, the boundaries connected to our concept of time and space are being affected by the globalization, and every human being is expected to practise the ability to co-exist and to co-operate across cultural and national boundaries. As a result of a smaller world everyone has a knowledge about how their lives can be lived by choosing alternative ways which furthermore changes the conventional concept of the normal life and the predictable future. This encourage and widespread the individualistic way of living. Several sociologists emphasize that qua these phenomenons and tendencies where everyone distances each other because of the individualism, at the same time the globalisation forces everyone in the opposite direction towards each other. More encounters appear as every society becomes more multiculturally. A main rule in this development towards each other is that our communication competences will determine how close we can become in our co-existince and co-operation.

The word communication comes from the Latin word *"communicare"*, which means "to make something common". Communication as a strategy and as a competence can therefore be understood as the bridge between individualism and community. The bridge makes the individualistic orientated people join each other for a shorter or longer time. In a globalized and multicultural world the demands to the content of the competences can therefore not only rely on making the linguistic competences common, e.g. where everyone uses the same language, but also on the efforts of developing the cultural competences so everyone can understand and interpret each other in the most constructive way, e.g. by creating a common knowledge about different cultures, values etc.. The demands are connecting to the need of constructing and creating one´s cultural communicative competences as well as common global learning skills and common shared knowledge.

"Seek First to Understand, then to be Understood"

The conception of culture not only requests to one but to several meanings and interpretations. At a macro-level culture can be defined as a *sector in the society*, e.g. music, art, literature, drama, sport etc. At a meso-level culture can be understood as a certain *life style or a pattern of behaviour* people use, which can contribute to create either a longer distance between human beings or unifying them, e.g. the culture in a modern city versus the culture in a traditional village or the culture of engineering versus the culture of medical science. Finally, at a micro-level culture can be defined as *frames of interpretations* which determine the thoughts, the arguments used and the chosen action of every human being. Therefore the core of culture holds the values one is socialized to carry and has internalized. It is with and through these frames of interpretations one experiences differently cultural encounters, and by using communication as a bridge, everyone becomes closer.

Thus several theories emphasize the impossibility of examining the cultural glasses one is using in communication and in interpretations with different cultures, Milton Benneth stresses out the importance of understanding the development of one´s intercultural competences as a dynamic process where a person is moving from an ethnocentric stage towards an ethnorelative stage and towards greater cultural sensitivity (Benneth, 1993). As the former Danish philosopher named Søren Kierkegaard (1813-1855) once said, we have to *"Seek first to understand, then to be understood"*. The quotation of Kierkegaard in the beginning of this article also emphasizes humility as a strategy and a way of behaviour when communicating and interacting with other persons. By having focus on one´s way of communicating it is possible to interact and meet different cultures without overruling the other.

Intercultural competences are therefore among several aspects about how to respect different cultures and values in different encounters, how to construct and make interpretations succesfully, and finally, how to communicate through differently communication styles and competences.

Therefore the results and the outcome of any interaction between people can be attributed the communication strategies and the intercultural competences used in the communication. In the following, I have made some reflections and statements in order to achieve this successfully communication when encountering and interacting different persons from a variety of cultures.

REFLECTIONS OVER A SUCCESSFUL COMMUNICATION

Enter the Communication with the Purpose of Dialoque

Before you interact anyone, the overall objective and purpose of the communication must it be based on the overriding wishes of dialoque and sharing knowledge and experiences. If disagreements appear during the communication, this is not the beginning of the end of the interacting. Behind every change there exists a minor conflict or a verbal disagreement, and that is why conflicts must be viewed constructively. One should not stay away from any possibility to communicate just because it seems probable that a conflict might appear, or one has reluctance to deal with another person or culture.

If conflicts or encounters between people or groups arise, it can be caused by for instance disagreements in arguments or misunderstandings between feelings and values, or as the result of several misconceptions of any given situation. Basically, the one experiences that his or her existing knowledge and expectations are being challenged.

In a co-operation there have to be a possibility to give each other inspiration and the space for sharing experiences and meanings, one ought to ask questions and make reflections over one´s actions of behaviour. In interactions and in communications opposingly interests and values ought to be interpreted as common shared problems everyone is obligated to try to solve or compromising. No one can grow or gain more knowledge alone.

The Social Aspects

Abraham Lincoln (1809-1865), a former American president, once said that *"When I am getting ready to reason with a man, I spend one-third of my time thinking about myself and what I am going to say, and two-thirds thinking about him and what he is going to say"*.

Everyone thinks, acts and interprets differently according to the cultural frame one possesses, and therefore the social aspects of one´s background, milieu and family affairs will interfere in the communication. These aspects participate forming one´s self-picture, and therefore it is important to bring this awareness of the other person's social aspects in the communication both before the communication begins and during this. Milton Benneth emphasizes that it is possible to draw some lines and perspectives to the way one´s background influences on one's thoughts, acts and behaviour in any given communication, and for this purpose he distinquishes between *a collectivistic culture* and *an individualistic culture* (Benneth, 1988).

The Academical Knowledge

Thus the academically knowledge everyone possesses influences the communication, this knowledge can be unequally distributed among the people in the interaction, and affects the balance of power. Whether the person is an expert or not in the theme/field of discussion, the respect and sensitivity towards each other have to be maintained. If a person really wants to help another one gaining more knowledge, he actually has to act in a humble way and take the hand of the other and from there lead him further on. The quotation in the beginning of this article by Søren Kierkegaard emphasizes this matter.

Everyone possesses different roles depending on the situation and context, for instance the role of being a mother, the role connected to one's job and the official working title etc., and in continuation of these roles different demands and expectations and the way of acting are attached.

In the following, four types of expectations to a role can interfere in the communication:

- the expectations a person has to oneself
- the expectations people have to oneself
- the understanding a person has of other's expectations
- the expectations a person has to others.

Because neutral communication does not exist, it does matter which roles and expectations every person bring into the communication because these influence the interpretations.

Cultural Sensitivity in the Communication

Do we accept each other and the freedom everyone has of choosing differently communication styles? Even though people interact through differently cultural frames of interpretations, everyone shares a common goal of generating meaning of the communication. According to Milton Benneth it does matter which culture one represents in the communication because different communication styles are connected to differently cultures.

Milton Benneth emphasizes that a direct, elaborate, personal and instrumental style are more often being used by people from individualistic cultures, e.g. Western Europe, U.S., and Scandinavien, where *"expressing complete, accurate meaning through appropriate word choice is important"* (Francesco & Gold, 1998, p. 31). This communication is characterized of an orientation of individualism by speaking their minds freely through direct verbal expressions. The norms of honesty and openness have therefore a high priority in these cultures.

The other way round, people from collectivistic cultures, e.g. Asian cultures, some African cultures, use more often an indirect, succinct, contextual and affective style, where *"(...) people do not rely on language alone for communication. Tone of voice, timing, facial expression, and behaving in ways considered acceptable in the society are major means of expression."* (Francesco & Gold, 1998, p. 30). Group harmony and conformity have a high priority in communication where imprecise, ambiguous verbal communication behaviours are being used. The demand of practicing sensitivity towards each other is therefore not only on a verbal level but also on a non-verbal level where the body language has an important part in the communication.

Distance and Proximity in Communication

A demand for making a communication successfully is the respect of different attitudes and feelings attached to the touched themes during the communication. This sensitivity is very important if the goal of the communication is solving a certain problem. A demand is, furthermore, the ability to distance oneself from one´s feelings and practice the competence of maintaining oneself objective and keeping the touched themes on a matter-of-fact level. Sometimes the goal of the communication between cultures is not making compromises, but opening new doors to new cultures.

If you allow communication to be a link and a bridge between two human beings it is not enough to remain on the middle of the bridge because we do not dare to set foot on the other's land. With communication we can make a discovery on the one's thoughts, values and attitudes for then to invite the other to visit your own ground and terrain.

Do We Understand Each Other Even Though We are Speaking the Same Language

From the science of linguistics we know that one specific word can have several different significances. Defining the exactly meaning of the word and creating a common shared understanding of the conception is therefore important in every communication for awoiding any misunderstandings. The clarification of a certain touched phenomenon ought to be practicing in every communication to assure creating a common understanding and interpretation for everyone. It is not a matter of course that everyone from different cultures, who is possessing varying frames of interpretations, achieves the identical understanding or meaning of the identical word of statements as *"using democratically organizing abilities", "creating the best school in the world", "the emancipation of women"* or *"a disciplinary punishment"*. Words or statements detached from the original context will be interpreted through both one's frame of interpretation, cultural glasses and through one´s values. The different significances of words can, for instance, lead to several people, who are discussing what seems to be the same theme or thing, but when we are listening closer, they are not having a communication or dialog, but having a monoloque instead. This is, for instance, very frequently seen by politicians. No statements are value-free, so when a statement is expressed, such as for instance *"a disciplinary punishment"*, the interpretation of the context ought to be right in awoiding misunderstandings, e.g. the statement expressed in a context with soldiers might seem more appropriate then expressing this statement in a daycare center for children.

Likewise, a linguistic word which exists in one culture might not always exists in another culture, which can cause translation problems when pointing out the conception of the word.

As expressed above communication covers verbal language as well as non-verbal body language. Often people who communicate forget the importance of using their body language in a proper, correctly way adapted to the cultural context and the situation. The way of expressing oneself using the body language is not only affected of an individual's personality, e.g. the difference between being a shy, silent person or an outgoing, loud-talking person, but also conditioned by one´s culture, e.g. Milton Benneth´s distinction between communication styles in the individualistic or the collectivistic cultures.

If a person uses gesticulation and talks loud during a communication, he can in a certain culture be interpreted as showing involvement, passion and power. If the cultural context changes this person might be interpreted as being violent, temperamental and maybe angry. Same opposite interpretations will appear if a person seems shy and communicates silently; verbal and non-verbal. In one context this behaviour is expected and is therefore interpreted as normal behaviour, and in another context this behaviour might appear as strange in a situation of communication. Self-consciousness, self-reflection and sense of occasion in any communication are skills everyone ought to practise and learn.

THE CHANGES BEGIN WITH YOURSELF

Our interaction and communication take place in the dialectics between the others and ourselves. Because we always communicate, conscious as unconscious, the overriding demand is about, if we wish changes we must begin with ourselves. Søren Kierkegaard knew this for barely 150 years ago, as the quotation in the beginning of the article demonstrates. An acknowledgement we all continuous must keep in our minds. But to create this acknowledgement and these changes a consciousness-raising of both one's communication and the competences demands, you interact with when encountering other cultures.

I have been trying with this article to throw light on the communication as the link and the bridge between the individual human being and the community. Communication also enables different cultures encountering. It becomes through the communication that we unify and through interaction that we can grow up as human beings–together or separately. The communication becomes the tool that can bring people and knowledge together and with that it creates development and a better world. But you have to take the responsibility of your communication. If you feel you do not succeed–try a new way of communication.

It is your choice
It is your responsibility

Remember what Mahatma Gandhi once told us: *"Be the change you want to see"*.

REFERENCES

Benneth Milton J. (1988), Verbal Communication Styles. In: Gudykunst, W.B. & Ting-Toomey, S. (1988): *Culture and Interpersonal Communication.* Newbury Park: Sage Publications, p. 99-115.

Benneth Milton J. (1993), Towards Ethnorelativism: A Developmental Model of Intercultural Sensitivity. In: Paige, Michael (Ed.): *Education for the Intercultural Experience.*

Francesco, A.M. & Gold, B. A. (1998), Frameworks for Examing Cultures. In: *International Organizational Behaviours. Text, Readings, Cases, and Skills.* Prentice Hall.

4

BI-LINGUAL–FROM EXPERIENCE TO COMPETENCE

Karina Louise Peterson, Denmark

Intercultural communication is normally associated with a form of communication where people, companies or organizations have to deal with other countries than their own, which often motivates to learn other languages and to learn more about other cultures and habits. But one can also grow up in a suburb in Denmark in a middleclass family and achieve intercultural experience. In my case sign language and Danish was the two languages I was brought up with. As I grew older I began to realize and reflect on the intercultural experience I had been given and how useful cultural competence is in many aspects of life.

I was placed in an intercultural setting from the beginning of my life, both in terms of culture, my mother is Polish and my father is Danish, and in terms of language, both of my parents are deaf and therefore use sign language. My parents chose to live in Denmark, so me and my younger hearing brother became bi-lingual in both Danish and sign language.

With the Danish language and culture I naturally had a strong community with all the other 5 million hearing people in my country, at the same time I also felt a strong community with the deaf culture, but with sign language my network was reduced considerably. There are about 5 thousand deaf people in Denmark, so that is considered a minority group-and a very small one in fact, but I felt that this group was much bigger since I had probably met or been in some kind of contact with half of them. It was much later in life I became aware of several facts about sign language and deaf culture in general.

Within the deaf community one feel very close and have a strong feeling of belonging to a group and network is important and people know a lot about each other, it's like a subculture, where the group in some ways is formed or at least gains its strength in opposition to the surrounding society. This is expressed in a strong self-awareness of the language, history and cultural background and being deaf becomes a strong part of a deaf person's identity.

One of the huge advantages of this culture is that it is very easy for a deaf person to make friends with other deaf people no matter where they go in the world. A typical strategy for a deaf person who decides to go abroad would be to locate where he or she could meet other deaf people, which of course is a natural approach, but on the other hand one could also question this extreme exclusiveness and preference of ones own group. When my own parents decided to move from the northern part of Denmark to Copenhagen, to live closer to me and my brother, it was very easy for them in terms of making friends, since they already had a social network in Copenhagen. Many older people would see it as a big step to pick up your roots and establish a whole new life in another place, partly because they are skeptic about the possibility of making new fiends in late in life. I know that this is the reason many of my friends parents use, when they talk about whether to move to or not.

I as a hearing person had "special" access to the deaf community through my parents and for me it felt natural to be among both hearing and deaf people, so when asked by my friends what is was like to have deaf parents and how I learned sign language, it was very difficult to give an answer since I never had experienced anything else. For me it would be the same as asking them, what it was like to be born and raised be hearing parents.

It never really seemed difficult to be in the deaf society as long as it was only me and my family, but when "inviting" people from the outside world into this context I began to realize that it was in many aspects a very different culture. I understood that there were rules of communication when talking to a deaf person, which not only was linked to what you say but also how you say it.

I then often found myself in the middle of two worlds and took the part of interpreter which in many cases was very stressful and as a consequence I often preferred to separate these two worlds.

When you grow up in a bi-lingual environment it takes some time and growing up before you begin to realize that you actually through your parents have achieved some special skills in terms of intercultural understanding and communication. First of all I of course had learned to use sign language but what I also began to realize in my late teenage years and as I got older and began to travel around the world was that I had developed an ability to communicate in a very clear manner. I was use to a communication strategy, where I sometimes had to explain things more than once and also in different ways. An example could be when I talked to a deaf person I could not just expect that he or she had "heard" the same things on the news as I had, which made me very aware of setting the context straight.

This awareness has also helped me when meeting hearing people from other lingual and cultural backgrounds than mine where I often take responsibility of the situation and make a big effort when it comes to understand the other and to be understood myself. When you are born into a family who belongs to a linguistic and cultural minority you naturally develop a strong sensibility towards people who are often not understood and then it becomes important for you to "help" and make the conversation possible.

Sign language is not officially a universal language, but compared to any spoken language, it's much easier to make yourself understood across nationalities. So in that sense it's probably still the closest we have to "Esperanto".

I have experienced this universal aspect of sign language when I many years ago went on a camping trip to Italy. Already the first day I arrived I have noticed that there were to young men who used sign language. For some reason I was not sure whether to go up to them and declare that I knew sign language as well, so I spent the next days observing them, which deaf people are very used to when they speak in public. Finally I took gained the courage to go and talk to them. It turned out that they were from Yugoslavia and that they had been traveling around Italy for a month without talking with anyone else but each other, so they were very happy to talk with to me. The communication went smoothly even though many of the signs are different from each other between the these two countries, the reason for that I think was that within sign language there are many so called "natural" signs, which basically are the verbs, like eat, sleep, walk, talk etc. and they are universal, those sign are shown in almost the same way no matter were you are in the world. Another reason was that we were very motivated to talk to each other and I believe that this motivation can really push you to make an effort to vary your communication style and take some linguistic chances. After my encounter with these two young men, I started to realize that I was able to make a bridge between two worlds that are usually separated.

The experience of growing up in this different environment first became a more conscious reflection later in life as I started to study and take an interest in sociology, communication and intercultural meetings in general. In this field I found theories that would contextualize my own experience from practice into a more general level.

One really crucial moment was when I decided to attend a summer university course this summer in Helsinki. The title of the course was "how to develop intercultural competence". This course turned out to be quite multicultural as the students came from all over the world and from many different academic backgrounds. To work with the theories on intercultural competence within this environment gave a great opportunity not only to experience and analyze the others culture but also to experience how the other students reacted on your own cultural habits and overall we were forced to look at this in a theoretical and Meta cognitive level. It sometimes felt like doing research and fieldwork at the same time.

One of the first discussions we had in the class, concerned the subject; stereotypes, and for some reason it became a very useful concept in many discussions hereafter. I think it had to do with the fact that we all felt the need to present our own countries and with that presentation break down some of the typical stereotypes which are usually linked to all countries whether they are good or bad. An interesting observation I made connected to stereotyping was that students who came from countries who normally get good reviews from the rest of the world actually felt the need to reveal some less flattering side of their own culture and for students who came from countries who are used to the opposite review felt the need to bring some good sides of their culture into the light.

This need to either defend or provoke your own culture is something I also recognize in the deaf community where people have strong need to accentuate that they are just as qualified and skilled as a hearing person. The difference though in this case is that the deaf community tend to define it self in opposition to the surrounding world, so in stead off pointing out the good sides of owns one culture it more becomes a matter of provoking the others, who you often feel inferior towards.

This is a part of the deaf society which I dislike the most, and often it has put me in a critical situation since I represent both worlds and that made me feel that I had to defend and apologize my ability to hear. This suspicion towards the others is often linked to the stereotypes we create when we actually know very little about each other and the case is that deaf and hearing people often live in very separate worlds and therefore it the fundament for stereotyping becomes solid. As I mentioned earlier, deaf people often seek other deaf people when they travel to other countries, which isn't helpful if the aim is to break down some of the prejudice and stereotypes there is on both side of the hearing and deaf world.

This point is of course not only relevant when it comes to deaf vs. hearing world, but a point which only becomes more and more relevant in a globalized world where we are forced to have some kind of contact with many different cultures.

An important aspect I would like to emphasize in connection to intercultural meetings is taken both from my own experience from my life and also from a theoretical point of view, made by Milton J. Bennet, is the importance of intercultural sensitivity.

I like the idea of achieving or developing a sense of ethno relativism, where one becomes aware of ones own culture and the reactions we first have when faced with other ways of living etc. what I find interesting within the concept of ethno relativism is that it accepts the difficulties which can appear with culture meetings and actually sees this a natural part of the human nature which gives a more honest and realistic fundament for developing cultural sensitivity.

5

SOCIAL COMMUNICATION OF THE MARGINALIZED IN ECONOMIC GLOBALIZATION AND SOCIAL MOVEMENTS: A FOLKS PERSPECTIVE

Govind Dhaske, India

INTRODUCTION

Social communication has been integral constituent of any social as well political mobilization that culminates in mass movement. Largely stimulated by the various folk art forms, social communication contributes in message formation, dissemination, and social opinion building process. The socio-historically vulnerable communities have maintained their culture of friction active through reinforcement of community values using folk media. Many social revolutionaries have used various folk art forms for social mobilization. Rooted in the cultural fabric folks art forms have been stimulating various marginalized rural communities in their fight for social justice. The journey of movement from scattered distressful experiences to an organized movement mainly takes constructive shape through social communication processes. In the wake of economic globalisation, social communication processes of marginalized communities have fractured systematically due to the institutionalization and capitalization of media. The suppression of cultural communication of marginalized community's folk media has been one of the responsible factors for decline in the social organization against oppression. The comparative activism among rural and urban communities signifies a noteworthy rural urban divide due to characteristic features of population. The cognitive inabilities of marginalized communities are mainly a result of the fractured social cognition due to multifaceted livelihood destruction, loss of cultural practices due to displacement, migration. The overburdened communication space by aggressive media is distressful reality. The nature and form of new age media and communication practices hardly contains cultural meaning for the marginalized. In broader manner, this can be termed as modified form of oppression as there is a deliberate attempt of overrepresentation of urban culture as compared to rural. The problem formulation in this regard is twofold; first, the rapid decline in the culturally rooted folk media of poor and rural sections and second, the incapacity of rural marginalized to organise and utilize new communication tools and media. The paucity of enquiries into various aspects of folk art forms and its role in social communication as well as community induced activism in the emerging development paradigm needs scholarly attention in the given situation.

SOCIAL COMUNICATION: THE CULTURAL ROOTS AND GEOGRAPHICAL AFFINITY

Social communication has been a generic process. To view the role of social communication in opinion building one can definitely look into the communication aspects of variety of community mechanisms established for community development. The social protocol mechanism inculcated in community practices to attend the annual meetings at religious places or the very regular periodic *panchayat* (meeting of social group under the guidance of *panch* which are elderly respected people on account of their knowledge and decision making capacity) shows the compliance to the collective. Based on the observations of the weekly panchayat of nomadic community

'Nandiwale' in developing rural diversified economic context, the author claims that the communities across various geographical parts within same broad geographical region follow the communication protocols. For weekly meetings in the central developed village, messages were disseminated during the week by various community members .this gets culminated in the weekly session of panchayat. These meetings are generally organized for discussion on various community issues, rituals and festivities and more importantly for conflict resolution. The livelihood mobility in the unorganized rural sector is root of this communication mechanism. It is significant to note that, the social communication among community members gets a prime place in the weekly meetings. The missing participation of women shows the gendered nature of community practices. This also shows the need of aggressive participation of women in the social communication process to receive some space and place for their issues. In the closed social context of a nomadic community, the loss of communication process inculcated in social communication reaps a considerable exclusion of almost half of the community members.

The isolated social functioning in the broad social context of social, economic and cultural diversity, such traditional communication mechanisms of a particular community suffers. The broader livelihood exclusion and in turn the communication exclusion on account of prevalent low human development status lead to development crisis. The traditional communication processes and the mechanisms are interlinked with the uniform cultural practices among the community members. On account of common cultural premises, the geographical affinity among various dispersed community members is visible. But in more distressful migration context such cultural freedom is deprived and the displacement from the traditional context may lead to more complex subjective and collective human development problems. The exclusion from media, in availability of community friendly media and deprived development profile makes the correlation of continued oppression and fractured social communication. The Major learning form this example about the role of social communication as community based mechanism of collective formation and social development; the fracturing of same due to livelihood forces needs projective emphasis. Though the community traditionally carries a migratory nature of livelihood the decline in the 'traditionalism' and resultant modified demographical features have to be considered.

FOLK ART FORMS AND ITS ROLE IN COMMUNITY PROCESSES

Folk art forms have their roots in the time tested and community devised practices. Most of the times, such practices appear amalgamated in religious or healing processes with remedial utility witnessed in the faith and belief system. The ritualistic nature of such activities is primarily the point of attention for scientific enquiry as religious amalgamations are result of acculturation processes. Folk art form in its purest forms appears to have a development function on various aspects including health problems; spiritual crisis and various communities trusted and desired social functions. Considering the diversity of function of folk art forms in touching the variety of development stages of stakeholders it is imperative to look at the integrated function of same through social communication pathway.

At a very obvious level folk art forms have cultural reference to the community value fabric. The integrated function with use of art, communication and gestures with use of music and other orchestration components, folk art constitutes a strong desired stimulus. Reinventing the ideal state of function happens through the stimulus of folk art form. The subtle processes involved in community building through folk art forms need thorough investigation. The primary yet important awareness of freedom of cultural expression strengthens base of the act. Further, various folk art forms act at various levels of consciousness with various inputs and reinforcement practices. It is an interesting to explore the correlation between the intrinsic motivational processes of an individual and role of the folk art's stimuli in the whole process.

The community level processes correlated with folk art stimulus have another significant aspect which defines the scientific utility of it devised by the generational traditional knowledge. This observation based premise needs to be tested using the modern tools but this surely does not contradict the obvious utility. It is worth noticing that majority of the folk art forms are peculiar in the timing of performance, appearance, message, media etc.

The pedagogical understanding ingrained in folk art forms performance has excellent scientific sense programmed in it. In rural Maharashtra, the noteworthy are the 'vasudev' is traditional folk artists generally visits homes in the early morning and sings devotional songs aimed at value building. It is a positive communication which has timely sense and advanced civilizational understanding of human learning processes. The psychological disposition receives a positive constructive reinforcement which has scientific sense to it. Similar function can be observed in the various other folk art forms like 'Gondhal' which is performed just after the marriage. The primary function of the "Gondhal" has been to demonstrate the nature and sanctity of relationship. The familial role taking after a major developmental attainment of marriage, this folk art form makes the right communication for transitional phase of households etc.

FOLK ART FORMS AND SOCIAL ACTIVISM: EXPLORING THE PROCESS PATHWAY

Folk art form appears as traditional communication arrangement of various communities but if seen in the context of nicely weaved social fabric, one can easily make out the integrated and mutual function of the communication form in social development. Social activism is a mutually agreed community action against discontent about the system mainly due to less incorporation of community interest and over representation of interests of certain dominant communities. The activism, in majority of the events, is community expression of discontent. It is interesting to see how the discontent felt at subjective level gets organized in mass movement and how communication processes take place in such event. The folk art forms have typological segregation in terms of their characteristic function. It is worth noticing that there are certain folk art forms which hold function of and about motivating community members against injustice. The subjective territory of discontent felt as individual level receives a strong stimulus through folk art forms. The pathway form subjective domain to collective domain has social communication aspect of sharing and realizing the collective disconnect and organizing it in constructive manner to form a mass movement. In Maharashtra, the role of folk art form "Povada" was well-known for mobilizing communities against the Bahamani invasion and later against the colonial powers. Considering the geographical limits of communities in grasping the volume of discontent, the folk artists have played major role in mass mobilization. The ethical positioning and community acceptance of folk artists and folk art forms has to be seen as systematic development arrangement. The role played by 'Kabir Suman' or 'Gadar' in their individual folk art expressions against the injustice or humanist shortcomings of governing systems has been demonstration of the developmental utility of folk art forms and their time tested and traditional knowledge approved place in social constructions.

At a higher psychological level, the cognitive role of folk art forms can be understood in terms of stimulus which has utility in facilitating the individual articulation and expression processes and further channelizing the discontent in organized activist forms. It is praiseworthy to witness the approach of folk art forms where value and ethical frictions are used as major tool to stimulate the subjective thinking. The realization of individual and collective value overlap in individual and psychological processes happens through folk art interventions. Art, in its generic form proved to be a natural function of human society aimed at multiple psycho-social faculties. Folk art forms are the heart and soul of rural societies as it is the only traditional media having substantial role in community development. The didactic communication approach devised by well-known saint of Maharashtra 'Saint

Gadge Baba' for community hygiene and positive behavior change in sanitation practices has been revolutionary folk art innovation. To summarize, the folk art form has multiple functions in social development, if social activism is considered as legitimate social action then folk art form is the scientific media in this venture.

THE COMMUNICATION MEDIA DEBATE: FOLKS OPPRESSION

The cultural freedom or in general the spaces for cultural expression have been reduced to considerable extent. The development vulnerability at broader level has become cultural vulnerability in the existing development paradigm. The primary reason for this cultural oppression has been the dominance of electronic media rooted in a typical 'foreign' tradition. The Indian context with primarily rural demography has been rich in its communication tradition but the new media revolution has been incompetent in incorporating same in their technocratic ventures about communication. The oppression of folk art forms can be seen at various levels through various processes. At larger levels the destruction of rural agrarian economy has caused human development crisis. The seasonal migration as well as the long-term migration to urbanizing habitats has broken the traditional livelihood system and kept the communities fractured and displaced. The loss of development communication due to these macro processes has long term impact. Here, one point is to be highlighted is that the urbanization or any other positive migration can assure cultural freedom and places but the distressful forms are detrimental to the communication media and its cultural roots.

The inability of modern communication establishments in understanding the folk art and its community development function has been obvious considering the nature of media and its exclusionary nature. Instead of pitching modern communications in innovative manner, a communication over representation has been seen in the existing forms. The prevalent lack of researches on folk art forms and the psychosocial functions has contributed on less knowledge production for modern media development. The modernization phenomenon introduced through the process of acculturation appears to be negative due to its exclusionary processes on culturally rooted development communication of majority of the social groups holding distinct cultural identity and a human development profile.

THE ECONOMIC GLOBALIZATION AND MODIFIED COMMUNICATION MARGINALIZATION

Globalization has been a reality. Precisely the 'economic' nature of globalization shows its lack of organic footing in terms of establishment of multi-cultural interfaces in secular manner. The domestic development processes affected in significant manner due to economic globalization. The major demographic shift witnessed in India is about eth urbanization. The promotion of urban centric growth models promoted due to globalization forces caused fracturing of rural hinterland and its folks. The displacements and artificially stimulated development processes caused development fracturing of rural communities and the prevalent rural marginalization received a global dimension. The modified forms of oppression are visible in media and communication field with overrepresentation of urban media and culture in all content. Media instead of redefining its people centeredness created a demographic bias which has led to communication disparity.

The epistemological constraints ruling the urban based media activity are detrimental to the cultural freedom of rural community with tremendous socio-cultural diversity. It can be said that the urban cultural freedom is rights based action but considering the demographic oppression and counter effect of practice of one freedom, it is necessary to understand and act against the oppression. The capitalization of media fuelled the urban centric nature of development processes. At subtle level, the awareness about communication oppression is less due over occupied cognitive spheres and lack of immediate cultural reference. The marginilaisation, in this regard has to be viewed for constructive actions against communication disparity. The economic forces are going to fuel the ongoing process as the urban consumer base and the rapid urbanization process has been considered as major tools for profit making. The to and fro function of economic processes with human development and cultural freedom has caused the damage of rich folk-art tradition induced development communication.

SOCIAL MOVEMENT FORMATION: SOME COMMUNICATION CHALLENGES

Social movements are sign of healthy democratic function of nation-state. India being world's largest democracy holds a special place among the global reformist intellectuals due to its rich democratic culture and consequent social tools like folk art forms. With the rapid pace of globalization, there are multiple forms of oppression emerging. The civil action through vigilant community remains a challenge for development functionaries. The twofold challenges in this regard are the awareness creation among various excluded communities as well as action against the oppression. Both actions involve magnificent and innovative role of communication processes. The existing media conditioning has been creating a particular cognitive fracturing which affects the subjective and in turn collective rationality. The major challenge of development communication is not just facilitating and stimulating social communication but to creating awareness about the negative communication forms aimed at vested interests of oppressive forces. Reinventing the traditional media and utilizing same in innovative manner remains challenge. This signifies an in-depth research on folk art forms and the traditional development communication media.

Social movements as a collective reaction against injustice or need of reform are generic functions of human civilization. The movement formation process among the users of technocratic population groups appears very competent on information dissemination front but the definite miss of 'collective' feelings can be referred to the lack of integration of advanced value fabric behind the emergence of folk art forms as community media. The communication challenges for new social movements are challenges of appealing to the sensitivity. The value shift brought about by the oppressive and biased development processes is the challenges. The communication challenges in this regard are multifaceted and multidimensional.

Section–II

Art and Literature

6

KATHAKALI: CULTURAL EXTRAVAGANZA FROM THE GOD'S OWN COUNTRY

Prema Ramachandran, India

Kathakali is a highly stylized form of dance drama, which originated in the God's own country i.e. Kerala. Kerala has a rich tradition of ritual and folk art forms, which helped in propagating the collective cultural heritage of the state even in the days before literacy became prevalent in the state. It is a prime example of effective and efficient communication. The name Kathakali is derived from the combination of two Malayalam words *katha,* which means story, and *kali,* which means play. Kathakali narrates selected stories from Hindu mythology using detailed hand gestures called *mudras,* stylized dancing and background vocal music. The highly colorful and distinctive facial makeup, costumes that are elaborately meticulous from the waist up and curiously colorless below the waist, bestows a unique quality on this art form. Accompanied by '*chenda*' (a type of drum) and *chengila* (a metal gong struck with a wooden stick to produce a booming noise), *maddalam*(a set of percussion instruments which is played by tapping the fingers of both hands against a tightly stretched piece of animal skin)and *edakka* (a smaller percussion instrument)and supported by the singers who sing the story composed in verse and set to music, Kathakali is a combination of visual, vocal and verbal components and a veritable feast for all the senses.

ORIGIN

Kathakali is widely believed to have originated in Kerala in the 16th century A.D. The ruler of the small province Kottarakkara is credited with evolving Kathakali from the elements of two popular temple art forms of the day, Ramanattam and Krishanattam. These were vehicles for the stories of Hindu deities Rama and Krishna respectively. Traces of other ritualistic art forms like *theyyam, theeyattam, koodiyattam, padayani* and the martial art of Kerala called *kalarippayattu* can also be discerned in the dancing, acting and body language of Kathakali. Legend has it that the Thampuran (ruler) of Kottarakkara province wanted to have Ramanattam performed in his palace, but was refused on the ground that it can only be performed within temple precincts. Miffed at this perceived slight, he went on to combine the popular art forms of the day into a distinctive new form which surpassed its sources in visual artistry and imaginative presentation. The language of Kathakali literature is a unique amalgamation of Sanskrit and Malayalam words called *manipravalam,* which literally means a conjunction of rubies and corals.

HISTORY

A renowned Sanskrit scholar of the 18th century, Kaplingad Narayanan Namboodiri, is credited with refining the choreography of Kathakali. There is an interesting folklore about its costumes, which is a curious combination of the highly detailed and colorful upper half and simple almost commonplace lower half. The popular belief is that the Kathakali costumes were revealed by divine intervention in a dream. The characters were shown in the dream to be rising out of the sea, and only the upper half of the bodies and hence the costumes were visible above the water. Nobody dared to add anything to the divine revelation and the invisible lower half was made up of traditional white clothing, the same for all characters. Traditionally performed in temples, palaces or homes of the aristocracy, Kathakali has now come out of the ivory tower and is now being recognized as an entertainment form for the masses. During the mid 20th century, thanks to the efforts of the famous Malayalam poet Vallathol Narayana Menon, Kathakali has aquired a more plebian face and is enjoyed now even by those who are not proficient in Sanskrit. Vallathol took it upon himself to familiarize Kathakali to all who can enjoy art in its myriad forms and established Kerala Kala Mandalam-a training and research center for Kathakali artists and afficiandos. Through the efforts of Kalamandalam, Kathakali has become well known all over with regular performances by highly trained artists. Most of the famous artists and singers had their beginning at Kalamandalam and often use Kalamandalam (now a deemed university) as prefix to their names to highlight their association with this novel institution. Other Kathakali Schools, which nurtured this art form, are Unnai Warrier Kathakali Yogam and Kottakkal Kathakali Sangham. Kathakali has become the face of Kerala to the average Indian who enjoys still scenes from the art form on pageants and floats and decorates the walls of his home with colorful painted masks of the important characters.

COMPONENTS OF KATHAKALI

Kathakali consists of the aesthetically and artistically pleasing mix of five components:

Natyam, which broadly means acting which consists of the innumerable facial expressions, which have been designated to portray the vast range and every shade of human emotions;

Nritham, which means dance, consisting of the stylized steps and body movement;

Nrithyam which mean the process of communication using the hand gestures or 'hastha mudras' to enact the story;

Geetham meaning the vocal accompaniment; and

Vadyam the accompaniment on chenda and chengila.

PERFORMANCE

Kathakali has traditionally been performed over the course of a whole night. The performance is designed to last for 6 to 7 hours, as the story slowly builds up and move towards the climax. This also gave the margin for the actors to indulge in their own interpretations of the situation (called *manodharmam*) and thus adds another plane to the story, which became the actor's trademark. This practice is now disappearing since the audience is too busy to sit, watch and enjoy the performance for a whole night. The *instant* variety of today generally wraps up in 3-4 hours.

Kathakali depends almost solely on the actor's ability to convey the story by interpreting the story using mudras, facial expressions and stylized body movements. There is, as such, no set or backdrop to the art form and the actor is the only resource, which can be used to create the ambiences necessary. The story could be set in different locales as palaces, forests or battlefields, but it is all projected through the actor's skill in using the mudras and expressions to the best effect. The few props used for the performance are the *thirasseela* and *Kalivilakku*. The *thirasseela* is a curtain about four by five on which concentric rectangles are painted. Two assistants and the actor starts off hold it aloft in the beginning of the performance by performing from behind this curtain and gradually the curtain rises.

The *Kalivilakku* is a huge bronze lamp, which produced the lighting for the stage before the advent of electricity and stage lighting. It is also supposed to represent Lord Agni, in whose presence all auspicious activities should take place. It is usually about one meter high and has wicks made of strips of cloth, of which five are lighted facing five directions.

A stool doubles as a throne or any other seating as required. The actors climb up on it to indicate a high-slung vehicle like a chariot.

THE SEQUENCE

Kathakali is meant to be performed in front of a large audience. There are many levels of enjoyment possible based on one's knowledge of Sanskrit, understanding of Hindu mythological stories and ability to discern the meaning of the *hastha mudras* and the portrayal of the nine *rasasams* or basic emotions expressed through facial expressions and rigorous schooling of muscles. Even without a detailed knowledge of any of the above, Kathakali still can be and is enjoyed by many because it is a highly visual art which mesmerizes with the whole world created right before our eyes using the minimum of props or aids. There is little to distract the audience from the direct communion with the actor or the character he portrays, so much so that the audience become a part of the magical transient reality created by the seamless and smooth congruence of the highly trained actor and the trained singer and the accompaniment.

A percussion concert involving the *Chenda, Maddalam, Ilathalam and Chengila* is performed before sunset in the evening of the performance. This is called *keli.* This is used to inform the general public that there will be a Kathakali performance that night. Reminiscent of the tribal drums, which carried messages across large distances, this is a very effective and economic method of communication.

Around eight o'clock in the late evening (coinciding with the conclusion of the last rituals of the day in the temple), the *Kalivilakku* is lighted with a wick, which in turn is lighted from the lamp in the green room. After the *arangukeli* which is a brief instrumental interlude involving the *Maddalam* and *Chengila* the curtain is held aloft by two people and *Vandanashlokam,* a musical offering to praise the deities and ask for their blessings is performed by the singers. Now comes one or more junior artists, made up and costumed in the traditional Kathakali costumes, and perform a stylized dance while remaining behind the curtains with accompaniment from the singers. Now it is time for *Purappad,* or the beginning of the journey. From this point *Chenda* also joins the instruments in the background. Originally conceived as a device to start of the play in the tradition of the Sanskrit drama, by giving the audience a clue about what is to come to whet their curiosity and increase anticipation, *Purappad* has now become a ritual performed by junior artists. The actors represent Krishna, sometimes accompanied by Rukmini and bless the audience and the performers.

Now starts a most complex percussion concert, which involves weaving a complicated garland of tunes and rhythms. This is called *Melappadam* and can bring exquisite enjoyment to those who are connoisseurs of music. The highly involved structure is built up by the singers using lyrics from Jayadeva's Geethagovindam and percussionists who complement each other and build upon each other's mastery and skill to construct a musical structure of unparalleled beauty and intricacy. After the *Melappadam* the actual performance begins. If the main character is one of inherent daring and stature, his attire will be called a *Kathi* vesham and when *Kathi* makes the first entry it will follow a ritual called *Thiranottam,* which literally mean looking over the curtain. The *Kathi* vesham will not directly come on stage but will keep looking over the curtain while performing his dance steps to give the audience a chance to get acquainted with the impact of the character in a phased manner.

During the performance at certain points the actor would follow the practice called *cholliyattam.* Here the actor translates into sign language the lyrical dialogues sung in the background. A reasonable knowledge of the language of *mudras* is necessary to really enjoy this part of the performance and hence this is not for the casual audience. Romantic scenes are enacted in a very leisurely and detailed manner where each word is translated into *mudras.* While making the scene quite sensuous this can slow the tempo of the play. More commonly seen is the *cholliyattam* in medium tempo, which is not quite so detailed. While enacting confrontation or battle scenes the tempo becomes fast enough to quicken the watcher's heart beat. When the accompanying music finishes a natural cycle, the percussion instruments give a subtly blended and fast paced performance called *kalasam,* which literally translated means, the end. The actor uses this piece to perform a pure dance.

The lengthiest variation of this is called the *ashttakalasam* performed by Arjuna in *Kalakeyavadham,* to mark his exhilaration and sense of achievement at the end. The *kalasam* is meant to be a reflection of the character's mood, hence the variations according to situations. Whenever a character is placed in an adrenaline filled situation the *kalasam* indicates it by mirroring the feelings through the percussion medium. This is where *Kathakali* transforms into the pure essence of communication.

When an act is coming to an end or when the portrayal involve narrations, reminiscences etc, the actor relies solely on his skill and training to convey the whole bit to the audience without the vocal support of the background singer. This practice of the actor and percussionist performing on the *chenda* combining and relying solely on their skills to convey the message and entertain the highly knowledgeable audience, shouldering the whole responsibility for the performance is called the *ilakiyattam*. This requires excellent coordination between the actor and the percussionist, a sort of chemistry, which enables the one to divine what the other is about to do because *ilakiyattam* provides the actor with a large margin to indulge in his own unique interpretation of the sequence. It also demands the ability to use his whole body for communication and is the epitome of successful and artistically satisfying nonverbal communication. The oft-quoted example of the great Kathakali maestro Kalamandalam Raman Nair refusing to perform *ilakiyattam* after the death of the *Chenda* expert, who always accompanied him in the performance, is a case in point.

STORIES

Although, according to tradition, there are 101 classical stories, which are presented as Kathakali, there is a handful, which are commonly used. Some of them like *Nalacharitham* (story of King Nala) go on for days. The most popular stories are *Duryodhanavadham* (portrayal of the Mahabharata war culminating in the execution of King Duryodhana), *Kalyanasougandhigam* (story of Bhima going in search of the divine flower called *Kalyana sougandhigam*), *Keechakavadham* (another story from the Mahabharatha about the punishment meted out to the libertine courtier Keechaka by Bhima), and *Kiratham* (the entertaining story of Lord Shiva putting his devotee and ace archer Arjuna to test and finally showering his blessings on him). Recently the repertoire of plays has been extended to include stories from the Bible and interpretations of classics like King Lear, Julius Caesar and Dr. Faust.

Kathakali music, which started out as a complementary element to the performance, has gained such stature these days that it is considered an art in itself. The songs are in the *manipravalam* (combination of ruby and coral) style of amalgamation of Sanskrit and Malayalam. Most of the songs are composed in the ragas popular in Carnatic music, which are microtone-heavy. A strong influence of the plain-note rendition of Sopana Sangeetham, the ancient practice still followed in many Kerala temples, of one acolyte singing to the deity while the sanctum sanctorum is closed and poojas performed, can also be discerned.

STYLES

Kathakali as an extremely complex performing art has, different interpretations given to it by gifted artists and thus developed into distinct styles called *chitta* or *sampradayam* in Malayalam. The major original styles are *Vettathu Sampradayam, Kalladokodan Sampradayam* and *Kaplingadu Sampradayam.* These original styles have changed and evolved over the years to two main styles, the *Kalluvazhi* or northern style and the *thekkan* or southern style. The difference is mostly in the stress laid on the dramatic aspects and techniques and devices used for making communication clear, artistic and enjoyable.

Make-up

The make-up prescribed for Kathakali is very elaborate, distinctive and evocative. It takes two to three hours to apply and demand a high degree of skill and expertise from the make-up artist. It is called *Chutti* in the lingo of Kathakali and can broadly be classified into five basic types. These are: *Pachcha* (green), *Kathi* (knife), *Thadi* (beard), *Kari* (black) and *Minukku* (refined). *Pachcha* is used for characters with a mix of regality and piety. Most of the heroes in the stories belong to this category. The predominant color in the painting on the face is green, as the name suggests.

Anti-heroes, who are brave and royal but have a streak of evil like Ravana, are made up with streaks of red in a wide wedge shape in the green background, and this style is called the *Kathi*. Totally evil characters have a makeup in which red predominates and this is called the *Chuvanna Thadi* (red beard). Uncivilized and rather rough edged characters such as hunters (*vedan* in Malayalam) have the black color dominant in their makeup. This is called the *Karutha Thadi*. The shiny, glossy yellowish make up is reserved for women and ascetics and called the *Minukku*. There are variations on this basic style like the *Vella Thadi* (white beard) used for Hanuman.

Naturally available pigments and mineral ores abundant in the region are used to painstakingly prepare the colored pastes for the makeup. These are ground and mixed into a base of coconut oil to prepare the necessary mixture. Paper cut into ornate designs are stuck with rice paste to form artificial, enhanced noses and mustaches and to expand the contours of the face. A small seed like structure at the base of the *Chunda* flower (*chundappoo*) is used to turn the eyes into a convincing red.

Acting

Kathakali performance requires enormous concentration, a high degree of rigorous training, exceptional stamina and finely honed skill. It takes years of painstaking and meticulous training before an actor is pronounced ready to go on stage. Even then they start of with minor *veshams* till they acquire the experience and expertise to graduate onto major roles. How the actor interprets the character within the constraints of the directions laid down for the role will affect the impact of the role greatly because Kathakali gives a lot of scope to the actor to improvise. Rather, it demands that the actor put the stamp of his artistic self on the role, which is why many great Kathakali actors came to be known by the name of their characters. Since the actor uses his whole body to communicate, it has to be fine tuned to convey even the most delicate nuances of emotion as well as transmit the power of the stronger emotions like anger, fury or thirst for vengeance. This requires 8-10 years of regimented training which included *chavitti uzhichil* which is the act of giving a whole body massage by placing the masseur's feet on the prone actor's back and moving it in specified manner, exerting just the right amount of pressure. This is rather a painful exercise for the actor, but conditions his muscles so well that he becomes as nimble footed and flexible as any martial arts expert. *Kannusadhakam* or training of the eye is also a must for a Kathakali artist to help him use his eyes to emote in an astonishingly versatile manner. Because of the rigorous physical training involved in the conditioning of an actor, men in the minukku make traditionally performed the women's roles, though more and more women are learning Kathakali these days. It says a lot for the high degree of talent and training that a Kathakali actor possesses that many of them who specialized in women's roles could convey the most tender of feminine feelings with ease and grace.

The whole story is enacted through *mudras* (hand gestures), *rasams* (facial expressions denoting a specific feeling or state of mind) and body movements. The *rasams* are derived from the revered book called *Natyashastra* or the science of dancing. There are nine basic *rasams* called the *navarasams*. This is true for almost all the Indian classical art forms. The following pictures show the navarasams portrayed by the famous Kathakali artist, Kalamandalam Krishnan Nair.

1.Sringaram
(Amour)

2.Hasyam
(Ridicule)

3.Karunam
(Pathos)

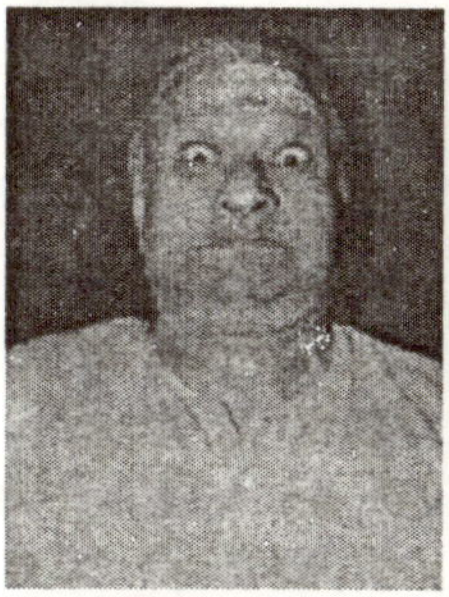

4.Rowdram
(Wrath)

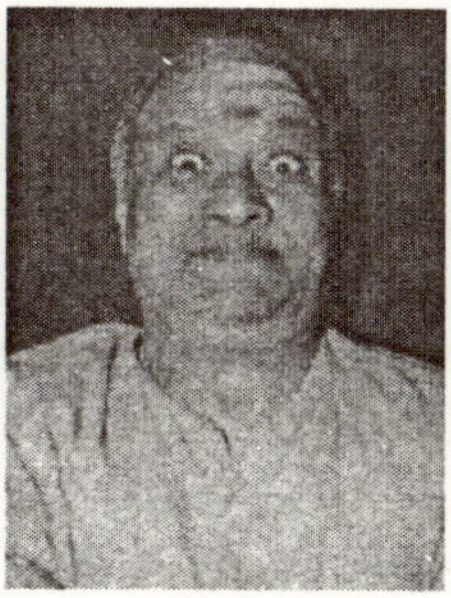

5.Veeram
(Valor)

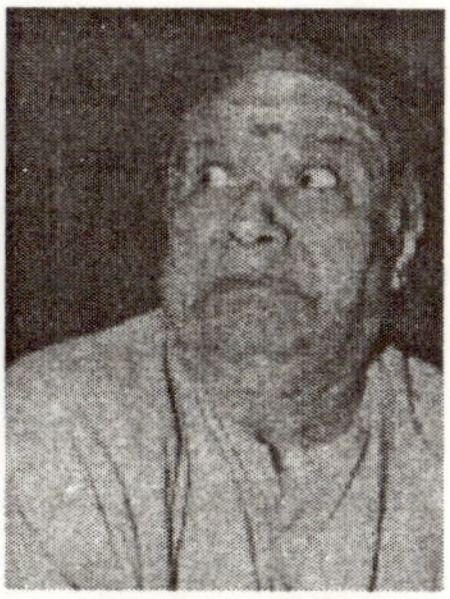

6.Bhayanakam
(Fear)

7.Beebhalsam
(Disgust)

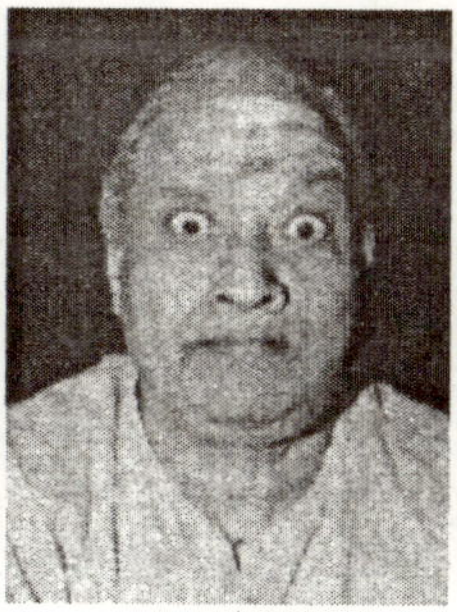

8.Athbhutham
(Wonder)

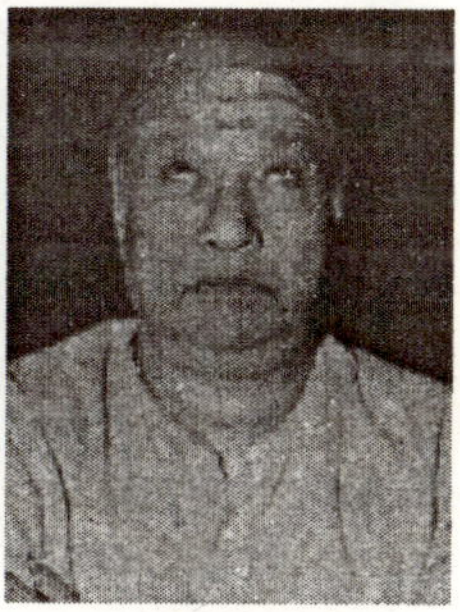

9.Santham
(Tranquility)

The *mudras* are taken from the 'Hasthalakshana Deepika', the book of hand gestures. There are 24 basic *mudras* and their variations. If only one hand is used in creating a *mudra,* it is called an *Asamyutha Mudra,* and if both the hands are used it is called a *Samyutha Mudra.* If the same *mudra* is used to convey two different meanings, it is called *samana mudra,* (similar mudra) and if both the hands show different mudras to convey certain meaning it is called *misra mudra* (mixed mudra). The 24 basic *mudras* and their variations together make 470 distinct symbols in Kathakali, which is enough to portray quite a complex bouquet of feelings and emotions. The following sketch shows the basic mudras.

Kathakali is one of the oldest forms of theater arts. It is a harmonious and unbelievably complex mix of many different components, which are individual art forms in themselves, and

1. **Pathaaka** (Flag)

2. **Mudraakhyam**

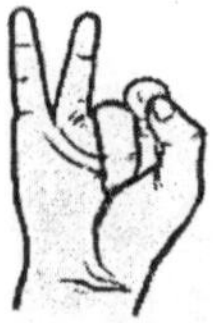

3. **Katakam** (Golden Bangle)

4. **Mushti**

5. **Kartharee Mukham** (Scissor's sharp point)

6. **Sukathundam** (Parrot's peek)

7. **Kapidhakam** (The fruit of a tree)

8. **HamsaPaksham** (Swan's wing)

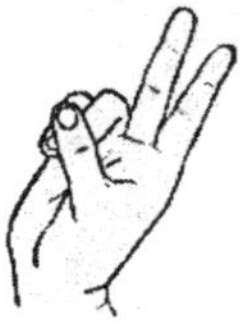

9. **Sikharam** (Peak)

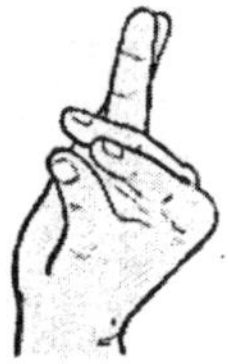

10. **Hamsaasyam** (Swan's peek)

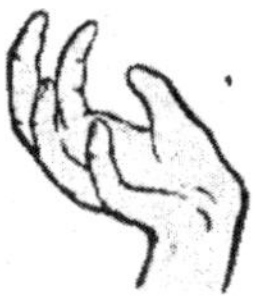

11. **Anjaly** (Folded hands in Salutation)

12. **Ardhachandram** (Half moon)

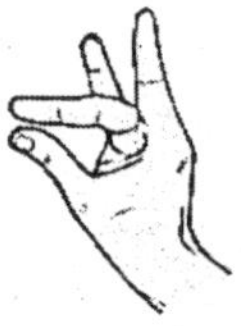

13. **Mukuram** (Mirror)

14. **Bhramaram** (Beetle)

15. **Soochimukham** (Needle's sharp point)

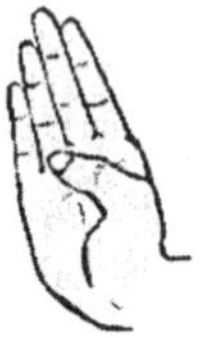

16. **Pallavam** (Sprout)

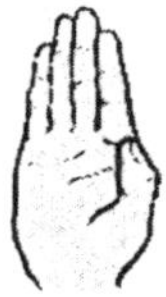

17.**Thripathaaka** (Flag with three colours)

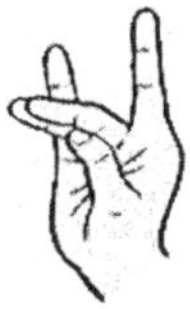

18. **Mrigaseersham** (Deer's head)

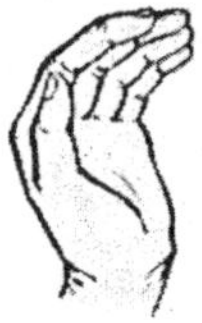

19.**Sarpasirass** (Serpant's head)

20. **Vardhamanakam** (Seedling)

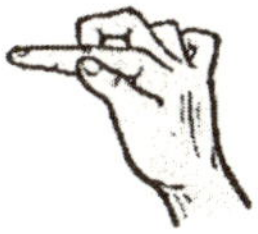

21. **Araalam** (Curved)

22. **Oornanabham** (Spider)

23. **Mukulam** (Bud)

24. **Katakaamukham**

is a prime example and proof of all the maxims of communication. The artist and the audience have no elaborate props or stage settings to widen the distance between them. By the mere flicker of an eyebrow or the minute repositioning of facial muscles a whole new shade of meaning is conveyed. The fluidity and dynamism of the actor brings to life what he intends to portray in obedience to the tenet of communication, 'don't tell them, show them'. Kathakali is meant to be enjoyed by the connoisseur as well as the peasant who has a casual acquaintance with the mythological stories. According to the competence and level of understanding of the viewer, deeper shades of meaning can be discerned from the performance. This is the reason why Kathakali becomes a passion to those who can appreciate the multifaceted nuances and grandeur of this art form. 'The meaning is in the mind of the receiver of the message' is completely true for the majestic, complex and stately Kathakali.

REFERENCES

www.cyberkerala.com/kathakali

en.wikipedia.org/wiki/Kathakali

www.artindia.net/kathakali.html

www.webindia123.com/dances/Kathakali/index.htm

Attaprakaram (Acting Manual)

Hasthalakshana deepika

7

WILLING SUSPENSION OF DISBELIEF–THE FUNCTION OF POETRY

Prema Ramachandran, India

The famous poet and environment activist of Kerala, Ms. Sugatha kumari once wrote:

'O my poor heart,
You look at the splendor outside from your dark prison
And forget all the torment,
You look at one star and forget the darkness of the frightening night
Bask in the sweetness of one smile and forget death'.

This is what poetry does for us. It shows us one glance of the unendurable grandeur just beyond our perception, gives a new perspective to the known and the mundane. It is like the landscape shown up in the sudden brilliance of lightning, familiar and strange at the same time. Humans have resorted to this form of expression whenever they felt their heart overflowing with the impressions and emotions that seems too much for the frail human heart to contain. In every group and generation there will be some who will leave their footprint in the sands of time by recording for posterity the variety and diversity of 'God's plenty' around them. These offerings in the lyrical format keep resonating with those who read them across the vast oceans of time and distance. That is the function of poetry-To entertain, to constrain the reader to think and to offer a glimpse of the private universe that the writer has inhabited, in short to communicate at the primal level. This is why what poetry says to one depends upon one as much as the writer.

If music is the food for soul, then poetry is the gourmet version. The poet who used this tool to communicate on a sublime level his privileged vision of the world assimilated the existing conditions, culture and customs and having converted them in the cauldron of his soul into a rainbow bearing his unique mark painted it into the social fabric of his times to be enjoyed by the countless millions destined to come this way. Looked at this way, each poet left for us an open window, which defies the flow of time and enables us to peek into the world, as he perceived it. In effect they left for us a part of themselves, allowing us to look into their very souls. This paper is an attempt to look at this priceless legacy, wondrous and overwhelming at times and try to decipher the messages so tantalizingly left behind for us, the future generation, to decode. A few poets who are appropriate representatives of their respective ages have been chosen for this endeavor. The way language was used as a tool to reach out to the rest of the world, the devices and techniques that turned the same language into a unique medium for each of them, stamped with their poetic persona, the cultural and social variables that impinged on a poet's conscience and affected his creativity needs to be delved into in detail.

Although all the languages which descended from the Proto Indo European language have extensive literary history, English has been the most widely read and appreciated. The flag following the trade had reached farthest corners of the world and made the English language and its literature one that maximum number of people understands and enjoys. The significance of English poetry increased accordingly and even well known poets like Ghalil Gibran or Kalidasa became known across cultures through their English translations. Since so many people speak the language the term English poetry denotes all poetry written in English, not just poetry written by the English or in England.

The history of English poetry starts from the Seventh century and during this period some of the most enduring and enchanting examples of the genre has come into being. The earliest known English poem is a hymn on creation, which is attributed by Bede to Caedmon, an illiterate cowherd. After the Norman invasion of England, Anglo-Norman became the dialect of the upper class and Anglo-Saxon metamorphosed into Middle English. In the fourteenth century works of English literature again began to appear. Geoffrey Chaucer regarded as the father of English literature and a worthy successor to Virgil and Dante made this century famous by his Canterbury tales. The Renaissance, which is credited to have started in England around 1509 and extended up to the Restoration (1660) saw a marked change in the reach of poets and their work. Because of the discovery of the movable block printing By Caxton It became possible to a large number of readers to make the acquaintance of poets like Chaucer and Gower. This dissemination of new writers led to the establishment of a native poetic tradition. The Church of England came into being in 1535 and this spearheaded the refusal to consider the Catholic Church's world-view as the gospel truth and more and more people began to question it. Along with these happenings the establishment of the English naval power on the high seas led to more and more adventurous exploration of the world, and subsequently to a wider understanding of the nature of the universe. All these factors impinged on the psyche of English writers, which reflects in the poems written later.

After the Elizabethan poets who largely followed the song tradition and classical influence it was time for the courtly poetry of Edmund Spencer and others of his ilk whose poems had an idealized courtly world as the backdrop. The sonnets of William Shakespeare also follow this tradition to a large extent. The Metaphysical poets of the early 17th century brought in a freshness that resonated with the readers through their combination of aggressive intellectuality with the lyrical formats. A few of the Metaphysical poets require a closer look.

JOHN DONNE.

John Donne can safely be considered the most famous member of the metaphysical school. Samuel Johnson used the term metaphysical to denote them much later in his work 'Life of Cowley'. They were not part of a conscious movement or school and were largely unknown to each other. His style is characterized by wit, subtle but telling arguments and the metaphysical conceit. Metaphysical conceit means metaphors in which the things being compared have more of a conceptual relationship with each other. To quote Helen Gardner "a conceit is a comparison whose ingenuity is more striking than its justness" and that "a comparison becomes a conceit when we are made to concede likeness while being strongly conscious of unlikeness." In Donne's poem 'The Flea' a flea bites both the writer and his lover and this becomes a perfect conceit to argue that the lover should not deny him sexual favors even though they do not enjoy the sanctity of the marriage bed.

'Oh stay! Three lives in one flea spare
Where we almost, yea more than married are.
This flea is you and I, and this
Our marriage-bed and marriage-temple is'

The influence on neo-Platonism is evident in Donne's style, and the theme that the perfect beauty of the beloved is a reflection and reminder of the perfect beauty of the created universe. George Lukacs the Hungarian Marxist atheist considered the metaphysical poets' trait of "looking beyond the palpable" and "attempting to erase one's own image from the mirror in front so that it should reflect the *not-now* and *not-here*" a fore runner of the forthcoming existentialism.

A strong intellect, combined with a genius for lyrical compositions containing rhythms which are more suited to the music of our times than that of 17th century shows us an erudite intellect mostly overshadowed by the façade of the courtly gentleman and that of the man of the cloth. His ideas were surprisingly scientific for 17th century. His credence that the world is, "all just supplies, and all relation" can be considered a poet's version of the theory of relativity. According to Donne the body is an equally complex microcosm of the macrocosm of the universe, which modern day scientists agree with. There is an unapologetic and passionate sexuality apparent in his sonnets and elegies whose unabashed eroticism leads to a contemplation of the importance and significance of experiencing love. Monsignor Martin C. D'Arcy states that not many poets have achieved more in the portrayal of "the full human person "than Donne. The defiance with which he stands up to that irrevocable finality of death which frightens even the bravest of the brave is not just a mark of his indomitable spirit: it also shows an understanding of the human journey that is truly religious in the real sense of the word and an almost visionary glimpse through the Veil.

Death be not proud, though some have called thee
Mighty and dreadful, for thou art not so.
For, those whom thou think'st thou dost overthrow
Die not, poor death, nor yet can thou kill me.

(Holy Sonnet X)

And then again, from the same sonnet we have
One short sleep past, we wake eternally,
And Death shall be no more; Death, thou shalt die.

This is the ultimate triumph over an unconquerable reality that defines Donne's poetry.

GEORGE HERBERT

For readers of the present century, Herbert is the poet who embodies the principles of the metaphysical school. Born into a noble family he gave up his position as the Member of Parliament for Montgomery to take the Holy orders. His poetry contains the quiet intensity of unshakable and serene faith with innovative use of imagery and a precision of language. His work bears testimony to the view that religion and intelligent reasoning are certainly not mutually exclusive. His poems speak of temptations, conflicting loyalties and faith and spirituality, all clothed in entertaining wit. His use of the metaphysical devises is clever but enjoyably so. This must be the reason why the religious poetry of a 17th century metaphysical poet has proved to be still appealing to the readers of twenty first century. Herbert has no religious ambivalence and believes firmly in the concepts of Heaven and Hell. According to Susannah B. Mintz, "Herbert accepts the premise of a fundamental instability in humankind, with the capacity for both evil and good, and emphasizes the importance of love and trust in continuing a dialogue with God.

King of Glorie, King of Peace,
I will love thee;
And that love may never cease,
I will move thee.

Thou has granted my request,
Thou hast heard me:
Thou didst note my working breast,
Thou hast spar'd me.
(1-8) Praise

ANDREW MARVEL

Andrew Marvel's poems are remarkable for its astonishing variety and range. Known in his lifetime primarily as a politician and pamphleteer, his subtle and limitless imagination combined with an intense introspective streak to produce poetry that surprisingly tries to reduce the gap between and redefine genders after the Reformation. He used musical and architectural analogies to eulogies the leadership of Oliver Cromwell as someone who possesses the traits for leadership and did not come to power because of the accident of birth. His "The Nymph Complaining for the Death of Her Faun" is an example of how Marvel uses the traditional literary language as a vehicle for a host of social languages like contemporary military state, Christian theology, The British state and the language of poetry which bears his signature. The Nymph's complaint serves to reflect the social disorder and chaos of his time.

THE ROMANTIC MOVEMENT

The late 18th century was a time of political and social turmoil for the western world. The French Revolution, the loss of the

American Colonies, a strident demand from the people for social change, less willingness to accept the established order as something ordained by God and an insistence on sharing of power with the members of the society resulted in an upheaval seen never before. Against this backdrop of change and unrest the Romantic Movement in English poetry came into being. The proponents of this movement attempted to express the "language of the common man", to bring down poetry from its ivory tower by abandoning the high-flown language of the Neo-Classic poets and the clever literary devices which were in vogue. They tried to convey poetic ideas in a language that is beautiful and which spoke directly to the reader's sensibilities and argues that reconciliation between man and nature was the essence of poetry. They planned to resurrect the 'romance' and the sublime that has been lost to people since Milton. Wordsworth classified good poetry as, "the spontaneous overflow of powerful feelings," Coleridge defined art as "the mediatress between, and reconciler of nature and man". Romanticism laid stress on originality and tried to find forms of poetic expression that communicated directly to the human soul. It is interesting to look at this in the light of the social changes happening around the civilized world and see how this powerful tool was wielded by the masters to achieve the need that every writer feels; to pour out his heart for the enjoyment and enchantment of the unseen companion, the reader. Some of the most famous and enduring English poets belong to this school.

WILLIAM WORDSWORTH

Credited to have started the Romantic Movement with Coleridge, Wordsworth was born in Lake Region in picturesque Cumberland. This awe inspiring backdrop of nature in all her glory contributed too shaping Wordsworth into 'The high priest of Nature'. He proposed the theory that poetry is 'emotion recollected in tranquility'. He reveled in the extravagant and prolific beauty of Nature but also saw as a manifestation of the divine truth which permeates every aspect of the universe. He considers Nature as the one Teacher man needs to learn all the moral truths and for him communion with nature meant communion with God. He used simple diction to express his poetic genius and succeeded in reaching out to that part of the human mind which hungers for beauty. Wordsworth's theory of poetry hold that the true purpose of poetry being the portrayal of the essential emotions of man, rustic, simple people are the fittest subjects for it, since they are more apt to be in direct and constant contact and communion with Nature in all her manifestations because of the genuineness and simplicity of their nature. He strictly held on to the view that language of poetry should bear as close a resemblance to the language of ordinary people and he proves in his beautiful ballads and other poems that this is possible without compromising his artistry or the beauty of poetic expression.

Whate'er the theme, the Maiden sang
As if her song could have no ending;
I saw her singing at her work,
And o'er the sickle bending;—
I listened, motionless and still;
And, as I mounted up the hill
The music in my heart I bore,
Long after it was heard no more.
(The solitary Reaper)

SAMUEL TAYLOR COLERIDGE

Coleridge who collaborated with Wordsworth in writing the Lyrical Ballads complemented him in his world view. Whereas Wordsworth believed in the simple and quiet forces of Nature and the connection between man and Nature, Coleridge reveled in the wonder and mystery waiting to be expressed through the poetic medium. He had no equal in giving expression to the strange and the supernatural and achieving what he refers to as 'that willing suspension of disbelief which constitutes poetic faith. The unearthly charm of 'The Ancient Mariner', the 'witchery by daylight' created by 'Christabel', and the Fantastic fantasy world of 'Kubla Khan' all bears witness to this fact. Though his output is small he managed to enchant the reader by the melodious and lyrical effect by the imaginative use of alliteration and onomatopoeia. The haunting word pictures he painted endures after centuries has passes which surely is the mark of genius.

And ice, mast-high, came floating by,
As green as emerald.
The western wave was all aflame:
The day was well nigh done:
Almost upon the western wave
Rested the broad, bright sun;
When that strange shape drove suddenly
Betwixt us and the sun.
(The Ancient Mariner)

WILLIAM BLAKE

The hallmark of William Blake's poetic style was his expressiveness, creativity and command over visual artistry. He considered 'imagination' to be 'the body of God' as well as 'human existence itself'. His works are replete with rich philosophical and mythical leit-motifs and symbols (the recurring one of God the creator as a blacksmith) which has fascinated students of poetry and communication.

Though he is considered to be a part of the Romantic Movement, in reality he is too individualistic of style to be so neatly classifies and has been called by William Rossetti a 'glorious luminary' and "a man not forestalled by predecessors, nor to be classed with contemporaries, nor to be replaced by known or readily surmisable successors."His antagonism to organized religion made him hit out against orthodox practices in the 'marriage of Heaven and Hell'.

Prisons are built with stones of Law, Brothels with bricks of Religion.
As the caterpillar chooses the fairest leaves to lay her
Eggs on, so the priest lays his curse on the fairest joys

He considered Jesus as the connecting link that enables humanity to reach Divinity once again. "[A]ll had originally one language and one religion: this was the religion of Jesus, the everlasting Gospel. Antiquity preaches the Gospel of Jesus."

G.E. Bentley JR calls him the stranger from Paradise who's Songs of Innocence and Songs of Experience juxtaposed "the two contrary states of the human soul", the two inescapable sides of the coin of existence. The sunny pastoral feel of the poems in Innocence is Replaced with the darker, heavier poems like the famous 'the Tyger'. It only needs to be seen how very relevant and contemporary his fear that children lose their innocence after exposure to the grasping materialistic world and its exploitation of them and his condemnation of religious belief that places dogma before the quality of mercy to understand why Blake has been called a prophet.

Tyger Tyger. burning bright,
In the forests of the night:
What immortal hand or eye,
Could frame thy fearful symmetry?

In what distant deeps or skies.
Burnt the fire of thine eyes!

On what wings dare he aspire!
What the hand, dare sieze the fire?

The Tyger

JOHN KEATS

John Keats is one of the most prominent poets of the Romantic Movement. He is the proponent of the concept of 'Negative Capability'. In his own words, "what quality went to form a Man of Achievement especially in literature & which Shakespeare possessed so enormously-I mean Negative Capability, that is when man is capable of being in uncertainties, Mysteries, doubts without any irritable reaching after fact & reason".

Keats firmly believed that poetic sensibility also meant that one accepted the fact that everything cannot be neatly resolved into satisfying answers. He believed that imagination opened for the mortal eye a divine portal of communication which cannot otherwise be understood. This gifted wordsmith has no advantages to speak of. He became an orphan early in life, had no formal educatio to speak of, no money to gain him acceptance to the society, was pilloried by critics who considered him an upstart of the "cockney school of Poets" and asked him to go back to his'plasters, pills and ointment boxes', watched his brother die a painful death which he knew was his own destiny still managed to produce poetry that makes one feel it is a rare preveilege to read him. The Englsh language in his hands became a work of art, a tool to craft priceless jewels that made 'every thing every place interesting'.

Keats's longest poem,'Endymion' reflects the immature and youthful world of rapturous sensuousness and almost unbearable loveliness. Its first line epitomizes the theme of all his poetry;' A thing of beauty is a joy forever'. He advocated the unabashed enjoyment of beauty with abandon. Still he come to the conclusion that' Beauty is truth, truth beauty' which is a remarkably simple statement of one of the major underlying principles of the universe. Keats' gift of vivid, imaginative and vibrant poetic expression was unsurpassed and his poems are treasure houses of masterpieces like:

The Music, yearning like a God in pain

Into her dream he melted, as the rose
Blendeth its odour with the violet.

Magic casements, opening on the foam
Of perilous seas, in faery lands forlorn.

It is the destiny of some poets to be not understood or valued by their own generation, but to make perfect, ecstatic sense to the future generations. Keats and Blake belong to this category. The bitter epitaph that he himself dictated for his tombstone read 'here lies one whose name was writ in water'. It is perhaps one of the ironies of fate that so often happens and a fitting vindication of his phenomenal talent that no other poet had as great an influence on the poets of the next generation as Keats.

PERCY BYSSHE SHELLEY

Shelley's poetry is characterized by a subtle and fragile lyricism, which combines with the poet's rebellious zeal for change in the existing social order to produce some of the most enchanting poetry ever written. He firmly believed in the intrinsic, essential goodness of the human heart and attributed all the desolation and wretchedness of the human state to the four pillars of established society, organized religion, formal education, structured system of government and the blind and inadequate system of law. This seems to be rather too anarchistic way of thinking but Shelley's sensitive soul found the inequalities around him to be unbearable and attributed them to the inequality of the social order. He was merely raising his voice against a church which forgot the exhortation to consider everyman a brother, a government heavily biased towards those who had wealth or rank, a system where marriages became life time imprisonments to hapless souls and a law which was blind to the travails of those whom it was supposed to protect. His much-ridiculed ideas were the product of a mind, which un compromising idealism was balanced by a skepticism born of his loss of faith in the established institutions.

This atheist and radical poet yearned for sensations, which helps him worship at the altar of true Beauty, which he considers a manifestation of the ultimate, the spiritual force that appears in the form of intellect and Love as well. His view of nature is diametrically opposite to Wordsworth's mysticism. His lyrical poems like 'The Skylark' and 'The cloud' hypnotizes and dazzles by awe inspiring display of poetic genius. His 'Ode to the West Wind' is an overpowering succession of swelling emotion and stunningly beautiful imagery of which Swinburne says, "It is beyond and outside and above all criticism, all praise, and all thanksgiving," The poet's impassioned plea to the elemental force to make me thy lyre, even as the forest is:

What if my leaves are falling like its own!
The tumult of thy mighty harmonies

Will take from both a deep, autumnal tone,
Sweet though in sadness. Be thou, Spirit fierce,
My spirit! Be thou me, impetuous one!

is one that many a shackled spirit longing for the attainable had made.

The trumpet of a prophecy! O Wind,
If Winter comes, can Spring be far behind?

The forlorn sadness and the eternal hope in the concluding lines finds an answering echo in the reader's heart.

THE VICTORIAN ERA

After the political,economic and social turmoil and instabiltyof the 18th centtury came a period of rapid economic growth and progress for the empire.Expandng Industrialisation and machanisation and successful colnisation helped to recover from the loss of the American colonies.Even on the political front the beginning of the process which led to universal suffrage began to unfurl.. The poetry of this era reflects the progress of change and new beginnings. The Brownings,Robert and Elizabeth are a fitting exampleof High Victorian poetry.

ELIZABETH AND ROBERT BROWNING

Robert Browning is credited with the innovation of the Dramatic Monologue and Elizabeth Browning wrote poem 'Aurora Leigh', consideres to be a classic of feminist literature, long before the term was coined. Theirs was a true marriage of the mind. Elizabeth who was an invalid for the better part of her life had storng opinions about the social structure of the times and was vociferous in her opposition of all oppression includng the slavery prevalent in America. She raised her voice for the rights of women and children and questioned the place of women in the world. Her poetry has a spontaneous rhythm and is generally intensely emotional and full of feminine tenderness. With all this her apparent carelessness of meter and rime is annoying and had made critics of later generations question the place she ocupies in the history of poetry.

Robert Browning's writing is interspersed with a subtle spiritual and philosophical quality. His innovation of the dramatic monologue is vigorous and striking and can be used with equal effect for both quiet reflection and ringing narrative. His portrayal of life enables the reader to interpret and understand the main forces at play. He has created an astonishingly great number of characters and in his interpretation of the poet as a teacher indulged gleefully in the analysis of the human character. But unlike The Bard who has innumerable characters to his credit Browning's characters are all to varying extent versions of his own personality. Browning's strengths are his originality and dramatic vigor, which will always ensure him a place among the great English poets.

WILLIAM BUTLER YEATS

William Butler Yeats, an Irish poet and the first Irish Nobel Laureate is one of the most important 20th century poets. The Nobel committee honored his work as "inspired poetry, which in a highly artistic form gives expression to the spirit of a whole nation". His early Pre-Raphaelite lyricism gave way to experiments with different ideological beleifs, "those of radical nationalist, classical liberal, reactionary conservative and millenarian nihilist" as critic Michael Valdez Moses says. He has a great admiration for William Blake who is, he says, one of the "great artificers of God who uttered great truths to a little clan" Yeats was fascinated by the rich store of Irish myth and folklore and his poetry is strewn with references to both, he was also interested in spritualism and occultism. His remarkable mind made him see things with a devastating clarity which made him remark after the long awaited consumation of his affair with Maude Gonne that "the tragedy of sexual intercourse is the perpetual virginity of the soul". Nothing can bring out the solitude of the human soul more clearly. This piercing clarity also held a mirror to his own actions and he was unmercifully honest about some of his mistakes. After proposing to and being infatuated by Maud's second child,Iseult he later said to a friend, "who am I, that I should not make a fool of myself?" Irish nationalism defined his poetry in the later years, as shown by his acceptance speech at the Nobel Prize award ceremony. "The theatres of Dublin were empty buildings hired by the English traveling companies, and we wanted Irish plays and Irish players. When we thought of these plays we thought of everything that was romantic and poetical, because the nationalism we had called up—the nationalism every generation had called up in moments of discouragement—was romantic and poetical".

His poetic style changes from the liquid notes of lyricism to the harsh modersnistic social irony and finaly to mystical spiritualism. These changes reflect his reaction to the growing pains of the young nation of Ireland.A common theme that runs through his work is the appeal that a life of contemplation hold for him over a life dedicated to action. His sexual exploits alwayse seemed to infuse him with creative energy and he is one of the few people who sem to have made the transition from late 19th century to 20th century with apparent ease. The poem 'The Second Coming' written in 1920 is vibrant with powerful imagery and seems prophetic when we look back on the past century.

Things fall apart; the centre cannot hold;
Mere anarchy is loosed upon the world,
The blood-dimmed tide is loosed, and everywhere
The ceremony of innocence is drowned.
The best lack all conviction, while the worst
Are full of passionate intensity

W.B Yeats' epitaph is taken from the last lines of "Under Ben Bulben", one of his final poems:

Cast a cold Eye
On Life, on Death.
Horseman, pass by.

Poetry is one of the most powerful mediums of communication. It bears witness to the condition of humanity, shakes us out of our complacent shells and lives,honor the individuals thought and expression, functions as a custodian of our collective experiences, exalts language from a collection of symbols to a living entity,in short "divines the human enterprise". The Victorians considered the poet as the teacher, who endeavor to uncover the hidden meanings of life. As a famous Hindi ghazal says, in a world where two and two does not always make four, poetry tells us it is perfectly acceptable to live in "doubt and uncertainty". Poetry is not just a vehicle to convey ideas. If the poet has succeeded in his role, the reader is able to come out of the prison of self and become one with the poet and look at his world through his eyes. This broadening and expanding of the human reality, which results in compassion and transformation, is the function of poetry.

The poet's job does not end with the transference of his reality to the reader, though that is what the accepted meaning of the concept of communication is. The poet goes on to the next level of communication by enabling the reader to go on a journey of his inner landscape, the journey within. This means that each of the readers works out for himself what the poet was trying to convey and naturally enough no two results need be the same. This astonishing power of words to mean, to symbolize different things to different people is what poetic sensibility is all about. Poetry transcends the mundane level of exchange of ideas and peels away the veneers of sophistication and experience that each of us wrap about our soles as a pitiful measure of protection. It forces us to decipher the meaning of the poet's words in the nakedness of our souls, where we cannot hide behind comforting platitudes, clichés and commonplaces. Poetry is a powerful medium of communication for precisely this reason. The impact of the communication varies with the strength of the poet's particular muse and the dexterity and skill with which he handles this tool. It can be seen in our quest to interpret the messages transmitted by these selected poets that the priceless legacy they left us will be enjoyed, examined, questioned, assimilated and decode in countless ways as long as humankind exists.

REFERENCES

en.wikipedia.org/wiki/English_poetry.

www.britannica.com/EBchecked/topic/1355021/*History-of-English-Poetry.*

Warton's History of English Poetry, Edited by *David Fairer*, Published by: *Routledge , 01/22/1998.*

Section–III

Reel and Ethereal

8

HOW DOES INDIAN CINEMA COMMUNICATE WITH INDIAN VIEWERS?

Rana Sinha, Finland

The hero discovers quite early in his life that he is different from other people. Life tosses him into strange circumstances. His strength, perseverance, integrity are all tried to the limits of endurance and even his very life is threatened. He meets strange characters in unknown circumstances and battles with deadly and treacherous enemies. Battered but wiser, he survives and eventually a path opens for him where previously there was none. This is the central element of the hero myth, which is present in every culture on the planet. From the earliest cave paintings discovered in India in Bhimabetka caves (some even 20 000 year old) to Bollywood blockbusters, art forms communicate this message of the human hero's courage, tenacity, and survival through mythological symbols.

Everywhere in the cities and towns of modern India, one sees cinema theatres, as well as posters with popular movie heroes and heroines. Movie stars in India get the kind of adulation that their Western counterparts seldom get nowadays. Place the plethora of Hindu gods and goddesses beside this vision of film stars and you have a modern myth of the hero-worshipping Indian. Are Indian cinemagoers really escaping from harsh reality into star worshipping and sing-

and-dance alternate reality that make them docile and passive?

In order to understand how Indian cinemagoers experience Indian cinema and how it relates to Indian culture in general, we need to glance quickly at the etymology and diversity of Indian cinema, the special characteristics of Indian cinema audiences, and the context of cinema viewing in India. Indian culture displays a kaleidoscopic diversity and richness of symbolism. As in all the other walks of life, the art of cinema reflects this astonishing spread also. Ever since 1898, when Hiralal Sen started to film scenes of theatrical productions at the Classic Theatre in Kolkata to be shown in Bioscopes, the Indian film industry has become a multi billion dollar international industry. In terms of the number of films produced, Indian film industry is the most prolific in the world. The Government of India, Central Board of Film Certification proudly claims on its website (http://*www.cbfcindia.tn.nic.in/*) that every three months, India's entire population of 1,1 billion people watch one of the over 1000 films yearly produced in 130 000 cinema halls all over the country. This means that Indian cinema does have a unique relationship with Indian audiences. People would hardly go to the cinema to be bored.

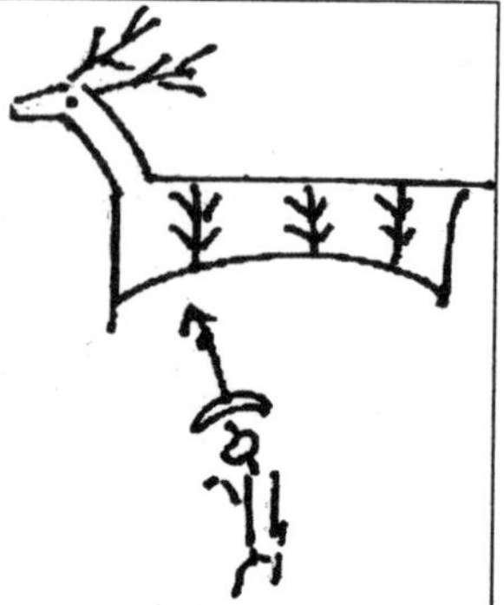

(Photo source: http://www.kamat.com/kalranga/rockpain/betaka.htm)

STREAMS OF INDIAN CINEMA

What is Indian cinema? Most people outside India have heard only of Bollywood movies. Bollywood is the most visible face of Indian cinema. Not only do you see Bollywood movies everywhere there are people of Indian origin, but in many Western countries there are Bollywood dance courses, Bollywood dress themes, and Bollywood style dance routines are influencing Hollywood blockbusters like the *Moulin Rouge* (2001). Indian cinema also has other faces. There are two ways of categorizing Indian cinema: by dividing it into commercial and art cinema; the second way is to label Indian cinema according to regions where they are produced.

Film critics also call the art cinema in India the "*New Indian Cinema.*" Basically, it shares the same fate as independent art cinema all over the world in having to work on shoestring budgets, finding their own sponsors from rich people, organisations, and government grants. Most of the early Indian art films came from Bengali cinema in Kolkata. Bengali directors like Satyajit Ray, Mrinal Sen, and Ritwick Ghatak were however, influenced by the Italian Neo-realism films of Roberto Rossellini, Vittorio de Sica and Luchino Visconti, as well as by the French New Wave directors like Francois Truffaut, Jean-Luc Goddard. In the south, Adoor Gopalakrishnan and Girish Kasravalli are also famous art cinema names from South India.

The 2001 census reveals 29 'languages' with more than a million native speakers in India. The Indian constitution does not recognize any language as the 'national language,' but it recognizes 22 languages in India, as the 'official state languages'. From a cinema production point of view, the multitude of languages that exist in India can be divided into two language groups; Indo-Aryan, which is all over Northern India (including Dardic languages spoken in Pakistan, Kashmir and Afghanistan) and Dravidian. Most of the Dravidian language group films come from the southern states of Karnataka, Andhra Pradesh, Tamil Nadu, and Kerala.

STUDIES ABOUT INDIAN CINEMA

Cinema studies in India have been guided by a Western bias. Excellent detailed studies have analysed content for ideological messages, while some have studied cinema as myth. Sociologically directed studies have either examined films as reflections of society and of social change or as articulations of identity and Indianness. Excepting a few excellent ethnographic studies like Lakshmi Srinivas's (2002) and Shakuntala Rao's (2007), one of the greatest shortcomings in Indian cinema studies has been that the Indian audience has been overlooked. They have generally been left silent on their seats as group representatives of gender, age or class. By failing to consider the manner and socio-cultural contexts, in which cinema is experienced in India, cinema studies sometimes misrepresent the messages and meaning ascribed to symbolism contained in them. The West-influenced middle-class analyst in a metropolis usually lives with an entirely different world-view and may misinterpret the organic relationship between the masses of Indian cinemagoers and the meaning they ascribe to cinematic experience.

ARE INDIAN CINEMAGOERS DIFFERENT FROM WESTERN AUDIENCES?

In contrast to cinemagoers in other parts of the world, mainstream audiences of popular Indian cinema adopt a very interactive style of viewing. The audience cheer and whistle, shout out to characters on-screen, throw coins or bits of paper at the screen in appreciation and sing along loudly with the soundtrack. The downside, of course is that some audience members also criticize a film or protest by booing or ripping up upholstered seating with razor blades and knives.

Cinema can be generally seen as a series of semi spontaneous interactions between its creators and its consumers. This interaction is semi-spontaneous, as no one really knows the magic formula of how an interaction could be accurately predicted to succeed for audiences. We know very little of the actual process of engagement with a mass cultural product, like cinema, when it occurs in public settings, in the West or in other parts of the world. The interactive style of Indian audiences allows an empirically grounded examination of cinematic reception for Indian audiences so that we can understand the processes through which the magic of cinema affects people. In the West, the moment the film actually begins, the viewing stops being a social experience and becomes a quasi-sacramental act involving only the viewer and what happens on the screen. In the West, the viewer comes to the cinema theatre in time, sits quietly when darkness descends in the theatre at the beginning of the film. Usually, there are no intervals and one does not disturb the viewing of other viewers by comments or expressing own emotions. This style of viewing can happen only at art films in India.

The bulk of Indian cinema audiences are regular visitors, who have an organic relationship with the world of films, actors, and producers. Indian commercial films differ from most foreign movies, as they cannot be easily classified into clear genres. Commercial filmmakers believe that most Indian cinema viewers love a variety show rather than a thematic narrative. *"Good masala, that's what I like!"* type of comments are common when people are asked to define films. An Indian commercial film would typically last three hours. This long viewing time contains tragedy, comic scenes, jokes, which make fun of politicians and corrupt businessmen, fights, family drama, tear-jerkers, slapstick and all of this interspersed with six to eight lavish costume drama song and dance scenes in fantasy settings.

A defining characteristic of Indian cinemagoers is the social dimension. Most Indian cinemagoers go to the cinema in groups with even children and the elderly tagging along. This family eligibility for films is also important for Indian producers and directors. *'We must make clean and decent entertainers. I shouldn't feel ashamed to sit with members of my family in a movie theatre'* (Bollywood Director Yash Chopra in *Express Magazine*, 26 May 1997). Unlike in the West, most people in India, especially women, would consider it very strange to go and see a commercial movie alone. Quite often the actual choice of the movie gives in to practical considerations like ease of booking tickets in advance, relative ease of getting to the theatre and coming back home and the area of the city where all this happens. Who you go to the cinema with also decides when you go. Urban middle-class workingwomen often see a matinee show with a group of female friends, but go with their families/husbands for the evening show or night show. Sometimes lower middle income-group and lower income-group men would go to the cinema alone, but they would construct a group identity by shouting, whistling, and talking to the screen.

The seating inside the cinema theatre reflects social class distinctions in India. The pit audiences, usually younger lower income group men take the cheapest front row seats in front of the screen. They are never quite, often throwing coins at the screen and shouting or commenting. Women are seldom seen there. The pricier back rows, and balcony seats are for the *'decent'* folk who usually dress up for going to the cinema and look down upon the rowdy behaviour of *'the lower classes'*. In India, even the 'short-length' Hollywood movies (1 or 1,5 hours) have intervals when everyone chats with others also on mobile phones, buys snacks, takes the kids outside. Indian viewers also watch films selectively. If a song and dance scene or a long spell of dialogue is boring, they go out for a smoke or tea and snacks, and come back after a few minutes. Some people are also repeat viewers and come to watch only certain parts of the film and leave when they've seen what they came for. Indian viewers seldom experience the film with the silent focus of attention that Western audiences do, who do not allow even friends to disturb during the film.

ARE INDIAN CINEMAGOERS ESCAPING FROM HARSH REALITY IN FILMS?

Many a serious scholar claim that Indian cinemagoers rush to the cinemas to escape the reality of their abject poverty and harsh lives. In the cinemas, Indians often behave as if they were among friends in some common drawing room. In India, many Westerners are bothered by beggars, dirt, chaos, congestion, and confusion, which they bundle as the *'miserable poverty of India'*. After experiencing the playful song and dance atmosphere of Indian films and noticing the carefree social behaviour of the Indian cinemagoers, these scholars are more than convinced that the only motive for Indian cinemagoers is escape from the all-pervading reality of poverty. Then the scholars decide that the only way to understand Indian cinemagoers is through the social philosophy theories developed in Western contexts to understand the misery of Western individuals.

The social philosophy of Theodor Adorno (1903-1969) and Max Horkheimer (1895-1973) theorised that popular culture made people passive, docile, and content even in spite of terrible economic circumstances. The social and participatory nature of involvement with cinema in India permits the Indian viewer to reconstruct the film, its import, symbolism, and message so that it can vary with each viewing context and is different for each viewer. Going often to the cinema does not necessarily alienate an Indian cinema fan.

WHY SO MUCH SINGING AND DANCING IN INDIAN CINEMA?

In India, learning and traditions have been passed from generation to generation for thousands of years through oral transmission. The two great Indian epics, the *Mahabharata* and the *Ramayana* with all their narrative turns, have relied on oral transmission even to this day. The *Ramlila* recitation, song, and dance play is basically the theme of good triumphing over evil and is very popular in rural India. Rich in performance crafts such as costume jewellery, masks, headgear, make-up and decoration, they depict the story of lord Rama's victory over the demon king, Ravana. The social aspect of the plays gathers crowds from all religions and audience participation affect the flow of the show. This colourful and rich multimedia tradition became the basis of cinematic storytelling. The advertisements for the first Indian talkie *Alam Ara* (1931), promised, *"All Talking, Singing, & Dancing"* as it included twelve songs.

Another interpretation for including fun and frolic in the shape of songs and dances comes from the Indian attitude towards religions, which is fundamentally different from the attitudes of the Levant religions, Judaism, Christianity, and Islam. In these religions, all of which arose in the Levant area of the Middle East, a literal interpretation of sacred texts, scriptures, edicts and sayings are the norm while in Indian thought a symbolic interpretation is practised. One of the most common pictures seen everywhere in India today is that of Krishna and Radha side by side as lovers. Now Radha is a Gopi, who is married to someone else. This does not create any problems for even conservative Hindus upholding chastity and family values. This is because the love, which Radha represents, is interpreted symbolically and is seen as the manifestation of divinity in humans rather than as ego-based physical attraction. In Hindu thought, the ultimate nature of creation is seen as Lila, or a playful aspect of the divine urge, which a pedantic rule abiding human graveness of demeanour and practice can never comprehend.

WHAT ARE THE MYTHOLOGICAL ARCHETYPICAL SYMBOLISMS FOUND IN INDIAN CINEMA?

Categories of Mythological Archetypes in Indian Cinema

Indian mainstream film characters represent ethical archetypes and not complex psychological entities, which can be analysed in the same manner as in Western cinema. You cannot have Freud sitting on the banks of the Ganges with Indian cinema characters lying down beside him revealing their secrets. Archetypes do not speak at analysis. They speak through you, but you have to learn to listen in a very different way. Why is this so? Because the keys of unlocking the mystery play of archetypical symbolic interaction are not in some analyst's trade, but in the layers of *sanskriti* or cultural conditioning and expression that constitutes you, the viewer.

There are six categories of mythological archetypes found in Indian cinema.

(1) The Hero myth symbolism

(2) The symbolism of the mother archetype

(3) Fraternity, which may transcend blood relationship

(4) Family

(5) The Holy man

(6) Eternal conflict between Good and Evil

The hero, who after all tribulations triumphs and upholds traditional virtues though he might rebel at times, is present in every commercial film in India as in most Hollywood productions from *Star Wars* to *Terminator.* Even in the angry young man genre of Bollywood films, which started with Bollywood superstar Amitabh Bachan in films like *Deewar* and *Zanjeer,* the tough and masculine hero communicates his feelings and experiences. This journey of the hero is not a trip to distant lands, but a journey towards coming to know his true self, and it provides a guide-map for the viewer to reflect his own journey towards becoming a fuller human being. Though there is no place labelled as heaven at the end, this heroic journey reflects for the Indian viewer the mythological journey of the victorious Pandavas towards heaven after the wars in the *Mahabharata* epic. No Indian viewer has any silly illusion that the hero or the heroine in the film portrayed by contemporary stars like Dharmendra, Amitabh Bachan, Shahrukh Khan, or Hema Malini and Aishwarya Rai are actually like the virtuous Yudishthira of the *Mahabharata* or Sita in the *Ramayana* epics. The metaphor of the transformative journey is not a direct emulation but a symbolic interaction. The real meaning of the metaphor for the Indian viewer is modified by an unconscious culturally conditioned interpretive process, which Western audiences cannot grasp easily.

In Indian commercial films, the ever caring and self-sacrificing virtuous mother is omnipresent. The self-made billionaire feels himself inferior to his poor but morally upright police officer brother because their mother has chosen to live in the poorer brother's virtuous household. The shortcomings of the heroine pales into insignificance as she attains motherhood. This is even quicker as she produces male children. The concept of *'Mother India'* started appearing in Indian films early on as a concept that can be seen leading toward a unifying image of Indianness. In the British era, local language films got away with using this symbolism as a vehicle for catalyzing national identity in defiance of British rule.

Siblings separated at birth but eventually reunited after scores of twists and turns of narratives is a hackneyed theme in popular Indian films. Everything is not smooth sailing between brothers and sisters, as there are constant conflicts and irreconcilable differences. Sometimes biological siblings become bitter enemies and a friend, or even a total stranger assumes the role of trusted near one. The concept of *'bhai'* (brother) or *'bahen'* is then an earned status, where human qualities take precedence over blood ties. This seems to often question the role of family as the strongest social unit. In a tangential way, some films also criticize the so-called watertight boundaries of the caste system and religious communities. A Hindu hero can find his *'bhai'* among a Muslim or a Pathan from Afghanistan can befriend a little Bengali girl, Mini, as in the Film *Kabuliwalla* (1957). But, one of the taboos, commercial Indian cinema has still to break is showing a man or a woman finding his or her community of *'bhai'* or *'bahen'* among gays or lesbians when their own family of friends have abandoned them because of their difference.

Family is the central social unit in Indian world-view. But, this family is larger than the essential mummy-daddy-kids centred round a refrigerator in a city apartment. Family in India contains grandparents, grandchildren, uncles, aunts, cousins, nephews, and nieces. This larger unit gives more possibilities for cinematic narrative to create infinite twists and turns for portraying a plethora of human characteristics. There can be a message that all religions can coexist peacefully in India as in the film *Amar, Akbar and Anthony* (1977), where three brothers separated at birth are brought up as Hindu, Muslim and Christian, and are reunited. Not every film shows that the family reuniting means smooth sailing thereafter. In *Fiza* (2000) a sister searches for her lost brother and finds him in a terrorist organization. The mother dies of shock, the sister has to kill the brother, and the family is sacrificed as the brother cannot abandon the terrorist cause. Some films like Vijay Anand's

Guide (1965) could question the practice of arranged marriages and challenge stereotypes by showing a man in a live-in relationship without being married to a career-minded adulterous and strong woman.

In Indian cinema, a clear distinction is made between people who are really holy and live virtuously and others who pose. A *tyagi* or *sanyasi* who achieves an elevated spiritual perspective and mode of action in life is respected. The *Guru* or the holy man is a common archetype in Indian films. But, this archetype is like a trickster. Quite often the holy man is a charlatan

like *Birinchi Baba* in Satyajit Ray's *Kapurush O Mahapurush* (1965) or Bhawani in *Sunghursh* (1968), who is a notorious thug posing as a holy man. Sometimes the stereotype of virtue can be challenged by showing a prostitute with a heart of gold, like *Chandramukhi* in *Devdas* (2002). MGM or Maruthur Gopala Ramachandran Menon, possibly the greatest star in Tamil cinema portrayed so many roles as gods that people made him the extremely popular chief minister of the state of Tamil Nadu.

The eternal conflict between Good and Evil is a spinal column of most commercial Indian films. The social order is temporarily upset by the actions of scurrilous and immoral villains, but the sacrifices, and redeeming actions of the heroes or heroines restore balance and order. The villains are always predictable and easily recognizable. In the beginning they establish a reign of terror like in *Sholay* (1975), but eventually the heroes, aided by virtue personified in self-sacrificing women, triumph and eliminate evil. The handling of evil in Indian cinema is entirely different from the horror movie genre. It is not something 'supernatural' out there in the shape of an alien but evil surfaces from within humans you can find in any walk of life in India. Stereotypes of scheming daughters-in-law, corrupt policemen and politicians, depraved teachers, immoral community leaders are used to explore tensions and upheavals in the matrix of the family or reveal various social issues like marital abuse, discrimination, suppression of domestic violence, or power brokering in politics etc.

Statistics and the treatment of issues in Indian cinema do not often go hand in hand. For example, in American culture, it is "normative" that about 25% of all American women are sexually abused or sexually assaulted (Dube et al., 2005). This "norm" does not mean that American culture condones or values that sexual abuse. Similarly, Indian society does not condone or value abuses that Indian cinema exposes on the screen.

Trends in Indian Cinema

Socio-economic changes brought about by the sweep of globalization in India, and by the rapid spread of consumerism are changing the face of commercial cinema in India. In the 1970s, the producers and the audiences could greatly affect cinematic tastes and presentation, but now 'market forces' of financiers are becoming more important. The tastes of the diasporic audiences, with their nostalgic views of Indianness and the differences in tastes of the urban audiences in metropolitan areas when compared to rural viewers are producing new kinds of commercial films. It remains to be seen whether Indian cinema is veering away from rural tastes and leaving the rural, poor, and lower-middle income group viewers behind.

Previously untouchable themes have surfaced in Indian cinema and have even passed censorship to be shown in India. Diasporic Indian directors like Deepa Mehta from Canada have made films like *Fire* (1996) to show female homosexuality in India. The two women, Radha and Sita, after experiencing bad marriages are caught in each other's embrace in bed by one's husband. The women lovers are not killed by a fire as in most early Hollywood movies, but happily reunited.

One fascinating outcome of globalization is the rise of regional cinema to address issues of immigration, success or failure in cross-cultural adjustment, disenchantment with new trends in society. Films like *Des Hoya Pardes* (2004) in Punjabi, *Bong Connection* (2006) or *Ballygunge Court* (2007) in Bengali are great films to fathom how people adapt to changing streams of cultural and social undercurrents. Though they might not appeal to the masses, they interpret cultural differences to people who may not have direct access to the 'other' culture.

REFERENCES

Booth, G. (1995), '*Traditional Content and Narrative Structure in Hindi Commercial Cinema'*, Asian Folklore Studies 54: 169–90.

Dube S. R., Anda R. F., Whitfield, C. L., Brown D. W., Felitti V. J., Dong M., Giles W. H. *(2005), Long-Term Consequences of Childhood Sexual Abuse by Gender of Victim. American Journal of Preventive Medicine;* 28:430-438.

Kakar, S. (1980), 'The Ties that Bind: Family Relationships in the Mythology of Hindi Cinema', *India International Centre Quarterly,* 8(1): 11–21.

Raminder Kaur and Ajay J. Sinha (eds.) (2005), Bollyworld: *Popular Indian Cinema through a Transnational Lens* Los Angeles, London, New Delhi, and Singapore: Sage, 343 pp. (paper) ISBN 0–7619–3321–2.

Rao, Shakuntala (2007), The Globalization of Bollywood: An Ethnography of Non-Elite Audiences In India, *The Communication Review,* 10: 57–76.

Srinivas, L. (1998), *'Active Viewing: An Ethnography of the Indian Film Audience',* Visual Anthropology, 11(4): 323–53.

Srinivas, L. (2002), *The Active Audience: Spectatorship, Social Relations and the Experience of Cinema in India.* Media, Culture and Society, 24, 155–173.

The Commonwealth Fund, *Health Concerns Across a Woman's Lifespan:* 1998 Survey of Women's Health, May, 1999.

9

OVER TAKING FAMILY TRAUMA LEGITIMACY

Abhishek Chaudhary, India

Entertainment, media, Information Technology and the great Indian rush are more or less the flavor of the season, not only for the Indians but also for the world. It's booming and continues to steal the show. The glitters of celebrations are all around, be it TV shows or movies. This study is an intense observation of the HINDI ENTERTAINMENT CHANNELS (viz- STAR, ZEE, SONY, SAHARA, etc.) and the Target audience they serve. The popularity of these channels is so big that it can be recited in Indian Entertainment History in golden words. The trend setting Saas-Bahu hegemony of Ekta Kapoor, The Amitabh Bachchan's KBC, Indian Idol, Laughter Challenge, Office-Office and numerous others have been the spellbinding success stories. However, if we compare the success rate with the failures then the figures can be concluded in one liner.

The Family Trauma's are always a success, the survivor. The industry is getting bigger and bigger and audience base is increasing in geometric progression, anticipating and appreciating, a larger space for more innovative and creative TV shows. But the latest trend has shown the shear depletion of creativity and artistic pursues, and have ended up being mere copycats. The corporations are making money out of sheep's share, trying to claim their supremacy within. Has the human resource concerning the artistic pursues died or it has also been eaten up by the CEO's while counting over acquisition and mergers or lost in cricket gully while bidding for cricket matches-Whooping 900 million US dollars for ICC matches in 2011 clears the cloud for all.

Perhaps that's just the panorama of the TV Entertainment Industry, as it seems to me. Now we shall move into certain details. My study has been focused over the following topics:

- The present versus past.
- The Time slotting by various leading channels and the analysis.
- Present Audience interests and the lucrative target audience.

THE PRESENT VERSUS PAST

The Family Trauma

Let's analyze this, TV is flooded by hundreds of soaps based on Business Families and their plight of marrying and re marrying, and again changing faces when need be. Even then these are the most sought out TV programs. The older ones are replaced by the newer, with almost same plot and vaguely defined theme of action. Now as we go deep into the content creation in most of these family traumas we find considerably no amount of newness. The trend setting Saas-Bahu stirred the Industry and then it was just the follow up. The quality of content has degraded to its lowest. The emotional quotient of characters is just limited to emancipated love, elevated jealousy, and certain remnants of Hindu family system.

Now if we go back to late 80s and early 90s, we find *Tara, Saaya, Love Stories, Dekh Bhai Dekh, Yeh jo hai Zindagi, Buniyaad and many more past successes.* These were, as someone might contradict, the past choices and today's audience will not accept them, had just one thing in common, they had quality content and strongly character driven story lines. The important factor to notice in these was the plot of these stories. These stories were not about some families who had a villainous woman, just the wrong women doing all wrong, conspiring and even killing when required. I would say they had something, which was not outlandish and were also not absurd and weird characterization.

One of the major arguments made by programmer of GECs (General Entertainment Channel) in favor of present content has been of target audience been middle class women who are home makers. But it doesn't hold any ground to the truth that in the past the numbers of such audience were higher then today's. I would argue that it has more to do with the inefficiency and lack of planning of these media majors. Since the economic condition of the country has improved the concentration has been more on grabbing the present slice of space. For example- soap on a TV channel has a girl who started out the love story with someone and now she is with fifth or sixth man, not settled and story is hung from past three years. The serial has been drawing TRP's for its networking programmer, and hence more business.

The chart topping and TRP rising is a very obvious result of Great India Boom effect and of some successful marketing stunts. The number of television set has increased many folds. To be very precise a labor man working in constructing a house owns a TV, 14inch color. Smaller cities, towns, villagers and other remote area of India have no form of entertainment, an alternative, except that they stick to TV at least 4 hours day. This moot point is very much visible as of why metropolitan audience is different to this hegemony. A larger and larger audience is being added every day, thanks to Tata sky and Dish TV, the TRP's will rise.

The soaps are no doubt the greatest fillers for programming in general. They are a collective way of keeping the audience stick to one particular channel for a longer period. Eventually it's an integral part of Indian households, but the question is, can the audience really relate itself with it like they did with Hum Log, Buniyaad, and also KBC. I found few old genre still lost in those characters and if I compare it with today's, rarely any will find a place in our heart today. Exceptions are always there. The time has really changed, the main lead of KSBKBT failed to secure any place in general elections, though her soap was a spellbound success. This era audience is intelligent enough to discriminate who is selling what and no one buy Cadbury's chocolates because Amitabh Bachchan is selling it. All in all the only point I want you to lead to is that- the future programming and advertising is not going to be decided in the flashy board rooms who are boasting and anticipating today's success as their own.

The communication pattern has been transformed from introspective ingenuity and badinage to baseless woolgathering. The effect of the interaction between the audience and television is not merely entertainment, it is has larger implications. Television is the major source of knowledge and is continuously watched. In majority of the houses it is the only source of entertainment and communication. In India literacy is approximately 65% amongst which the majority population doesn't have access to any other form of communication except radio and television. The literacy is limited to be able to read and write without understanding the relevance and implication of the same. This makes them highly vulnerable to the psychological exploitation through visuals. However fact remain the same that they have grown from that age where a good character of Lord Rama could become a political leader. Perhaps the absence of no other medium of entertainment and communication leads them to stick to the television. It may not sustain longer. The new lifestyle is evolving in metropolitans forcing them to switch towards the available alternatives. But that is where the gap is becoming larger.

TIME SLOTTING BY VARIOUS LEADING CHANNELS AND THE ANALYSIS

The morning timings have hardly been a sort after avenue. Shows in the morning include the repeat telecasts, music or religious programs. Various factors contribute for the negligence of the morning shows. Albeit the Sunday talk's shows were present in the past, now they are hardly in trend.

Considering the limitations this drift seems logical. Nevertheless some path breaking programming or technology makes a push. 'Baba Ramdev's yoga' had been successful to achieve that pinnacle. Few channels which supposedly offered as niche have also not done any significant work. The sleeping habits of Indians changed in the past, especially the odd working hours in the metropolitan cities, which is an opportunity, and can be explore.

The afternoon slots provide great opportunity for all the channels targeting the kids segment, and the housewives. Eventually all the channels get the requisite audience. Again space leaves prospective to explore newer target audience in the form of the former. This would allow the channels to achieve economy to scale rather targeting masses for broader audience base.

As we move towards the prime time the GECs fight for seconds, and that is where the real competition takes place. Numerous of them have established new standards for the programming in India. Since it commands leadership the media companies have explored lengths of it. Eventually the striking competition has recharged the creativity as expected. However it has increased redundancy and repetitiveness. The philosophy of mass appeal depends upon the quality of content whose ingredients were present in major hit shows including KBC and Indian Idol. But imitations of successful shows have further diminished imagination eating away resources just for the heck of improving the balance sheets. The possibility of a path breaking concept is reduced to minimum as lack of planning and proper research.

PRESENT AUDIENCE INTERESTS AND THE LUCRATIVE TARGET AUDIENCE

The Indian middle class is open to ideas and is capable enough to buy what they consider as worth it. Since it is the time of a nation under construction the usual ingredients need new thinking, a new outlook reflecting the significant part of who they are and what they wish to see themselves as. The younger generation is unenthusiastic towards TVs, and adapting yet newer forms of entertainment. A false imagery of reality may distort their perception of the true values they inherit. The media and entertainment, along with other communication has to keep up with their wants or else it will become foggy journey for them to accomplish. The depth of sensibilities need be explored to create characters that reveal them. The cultural diversity of India cannot be installed into one form. Moreover the inspiration shall not be in becoming Amitabh Bachchan or Smruti Irani. It should be the characters they play. Likewise the shows should be indigenous for viewers to attract them. A mockery of subtle facts should not be imposed to audience. Newer ways of looking at the audience are required. Not as a mere receptor rather considering him to be the king.

The successful 'Indian Laughter Challenge' has opened new gateways for future exploration. Same had been achieved by old tele-series of an enthusiastic girl's journey in becoming an officer in 'Udaan'. KBC may also be able to be linked to Indian psychology in the way it made the dream of becoming a Crorepati a national rage. Although programmers tried to re-establish the connection by introducing Shah Rukh Khan the host, it didn't upset the audience. However, later the shows made with the same theme did not work at all. This is a prime example of thoughtless herd following by and large practiced by all channels. Though some of these shows were an adaptation to western programs but they have been sensibly re made. The concept if not adapted according to Indian mind set and culture may have two repercussions. One, it may not be accepted at all and second it will influence the Indian psychology with western influence. Rendering vulnerability to the audience's perception.

The generations in the past lived in a combined family set up. Their lives were oriented more towards family values and relaxed lifestyle. The Entertainment options were also few with great level of homogeneity. However, today's fast tracked life is cluttered. New form of converging media is providing newer platforms of recreation. Perhaps the time has come to re-segment the audience and create formats accordingly. The concept of general entertainment channels may sustain to earn revenues from mass products advertising. Nevertheless this would also require new approach as competition will increase in the time to come. The new generation is exposed to the globalized world. Yet newer forms of employment opportunities are opening up creating divergent wants. The quality of communication and amusement calls for relevance. The success of MTV Roadies can be summarized as one such example of new age reality show. Since the Big Brother II has been reformatted and has been attracting a lot of TRP's, the future generation TV will require more uniqueness and creativity.

The buzz word is interactivity for the future. Participation of audience in choosing what to watch, where to watch and how to watch are cardinal for programming. Be it prime time show or a morning hustle the quality of content needs to be enhanced and improved according to the needs.

Eventually the segmentation into various new genres will require far above the ground research and real time plots. The educated nomadic tribes in various metropolitan cities are one such slice of people. To strike the right chord may require in depth analysis and observation of all these new breeds of people. The target audience is fragmented however the synchronized connectivity of converging entertainment platforms will provide significant return on scale. The presence TV is not limited to homes, it is now present everywhere; offices to schools, barber shops to airports. The marketing strategist requires going overboard to cater to these arising needs, and fill the gaps. All these efforts require a fine combination of creativity and marketing with long term vision.

With the advent of technology and presence of rich young generation a lot of Indians are showing fragmented heterogeneous fondness. The trends have shown shift towards alternate media like Internet, mobile phones, radio and outdoors. Perhaps the smaller towns are still relying on TV as sole form of entertainment but it may not continue long. The emerging media has started overtaking the existing ones. The revamp of radio is an outcome of the gap which aroused out of today's need. The radio industry is heading towards more segmentation and furnishing newer avenues of revenue generation. The integration of radio with mobile is one such example. This is further being explored in terms of a TV combined with the mobile phone. The question here arises is about the content. The user generated content may have captured a chunk of space through you tube but will it take the form of being the only type of content is out of question.

In the clutter of various form of entertainment forms, the TV would be more effective due to its wide spread cheap presence, audio visual nature and quickness in information transmission. The lateral effect of TV on the thinking process in the cognitive space further defines its impact on the audience and vice versa. The accessibility and less involvement levels of audience are sure to become its USP in near future. Computer and Internet may add further value to the medium if the message is synergized. The absolute negligence of the details, life style, and aboriginal attributes in the story, plots and dialogues may not last long. The presence of branded entertainment is also one crucial area which has not been explored till now on television. However it is reaching to that stage steadily. Congruence in lifestyle with entertainment will open more opportunities.

10

IN CONVERSATION WITH THE SILENT NOISE

Anuradha Malshe, India

It is so silent, the noise of us
The noise of people
Of men and children of women, of us all
It is so silent

But the shadows speak
The shadows hear and tell stories
Our silent voices
All the frozen voices of people
Of ecstasy and sorrows
Miseries and happiness

From Babylon and Indus
Till the ends of oceans and lost horizons of limitless skies
Cultures lost and found
Dreams buried and revived
Noise and more noise/
Lost in Babel, in gibberish meanderings
Confused souls of confused beings

Silent noise once again
Meaningful, poignant, pregnant noise
Dialogues and voices
Is it all clamor and clatter?

Once again our own din,
Of us and them
It is the world of sounds all silent
All still and hushed/
Muted whisperings on calm waters...
The Silent Noise reigns.

(*Anuradha Malshe, 2008*)

"In conversation with one's own self" has always been the best tagline. This one sentence is an axiom which speaks volumes and is always silent: is the silent noise of one's consciousness. Centuries and religions or more accurately spiritualistic faiths have been formed and reformed based on this simple axiom which is all pervasive in it's ubiquitous*ness*. Technology and development have made this inner voice of one's self rather weak, by smothering it in all the din and babel. However every now and then one finds it lurking out of a dark corner, beckoning the conscious towards the truer self. Philosophy of spiritualism is rich with meanings and contexts of these "conversations with one's own self". Here the canvass is not so rich but is rather restricted to Conversations and Communications. The path to be followed has some definite steps. From one's inner self the journey outward towards family and community, which ultimately reaches inclusion of a higher order is to be traced. This has always been an effervescent journey, punctuated by sparkles of all sorts. Communication reaches the highest order when one is oneself. The time honoured maxim of "being all alone in a crowd and in company with oneself", which sounds paradoxical at first instance rightly conveys the scuffle of the soul. Without journeying into the higher echelons of spiritualism, this piece will try to trace this journey.

On a more earthly plane, one can say that communication is ubiquitous, all pervasive, omni-present and timeless. Be it with one's own self or with the community. What differs is the message and expression. On more rhythm-atic lines one can say, we talk, we smile, we wave, we frown, we cry, we dance, we twirl, we whirl, we move and und so weiter..... just one thing: speak, talk, communicate, converse, chat and und so weiter.

Verbal or non-verbal, vocal or silent all this constitutes a transmission of message. The medium may differ so also the modus oprandi but still it remains communication with a big C. There is communication and then there is more communication. It comes out in different forms and shapes and also sizes. There are scores of definitions. One brief look at the internet yielded these many:

"Any act by which one person gives to or receives from another person information about that person's needs, desires, perceptions, knowledge, or affective states. Communication may be intentional or unintentional, may involve conventional or unconventional signals, may take linguistic or nonlinguistic forms, and may occur through spoken or other modes."

(National Joint Committee for the Communicative Needs of Persons with Severe Disabilities, 1992, p. 2) http:// *www.unm.edu/~devalenz/handouts/defcomm.html*

The definition of communication is shared in the Webster's Dictionary as "sending, giving, or exchanging information and ideas." And we "send, give, and exchange information" every single day whether we are aware of it or not. Sometimes we communicate non-verbally, whereas other times we communicate verbally.

NON-VERBAL COMMUNICATION

Non-verbal communication is the act of saying what's on your mind without speaking words. Examples of this include facial gestures (smiling, frowning), body language (arms crossed, giving someone the "finger", legs shaking resembling nervousness, sitting upright giving someone their full attention), and the impression you give to others with your appearance (dress, body image, body odor).

Many times the tone of your voice can reflect non-verbal communication as well. For instance, if you are saying one thing, but your tone of voice is saying another, then that reflects how you are truly feeling without speaking a word about it (yelling and crying while saying your okay). Many times we are not aware that non-verbal communication is a part of the definition of communication.

VERBAL COMMUNICATION

Verbal communication is the act of saying what's on your mind with words. We often take this form of communication for granted saying things we regret and opening our mouths before we think about it. Words can hurt or they can heal. So, it's very important to be aware of what words you choose to use when communicating to others as well as to yourself. (http://*www.relationship-with-self.com/definition ofcommunication.html*)

"Communication is a dynamic process that individuals use to exchange ideas, relate experiences, and share desires through speaking, writing, gestures or sign language" (Glenn & Smith, 1998 p.39). Communication includes language, speech and hearing and hence, a communication impairment can be viewed as any impairment related to these three areas (Sunderland, 2004). (http://uter.kambala.nsw.edu.au/cate_begbie/index.html)

In simple terms, communication can be defined as actions whereby 'actors' impart information to one another.

Communication does not have to involve language and does not have to be vocalized. (http*://education. newarchaeology.com/definition_communication.php*)

Two-way *process* of reaching mutual understanding, in which participants not only *exchange* (encode-decode) *information* but also create and *share* meaning. See also *communications.* (http://*www.businessdictionary.com/ definition/communication.html*).

Communication is all this and many more things besides this. If we make a quick sortie to the spiritual planes of the earlier para, one can glean the first step of this journey. Conversations start before birth, in the womb and continue in afterlife. In between it is interspersed with communities and inclusion and in more than one instance, exclusion.

Let's begin with exclusion. Let's begin by excluding more formal and much written about communications, like verbal and non-verbal, written messages, body language, information disseminations, technology, print, media and so on. Let's focus on the message, the between the lines meanings which nurture exclusion of communities and creates imaginary walls and also communities within communities. This is referred as de-inclusion, which is a function of reverse exclusion deinclusion of (reverse exclusion) for more mathematically oriented.

The process begins with social and cultural norms which become so entrenched in demographical psyche that they become inhibitions and later on taboos. The instances of these are apparent in all societies, irrespective of level of development or advancement. In developing societies, usually there is de-inclusion of women and children as also of the physically challenged and economically weak. Despite the best efforts of the welfare state this de-inclusion persists. The major medium is language which perpetuates the feudal mindset in an altered form. Indian society has been a bane of this kind for long. Colonization which is a supreme example of exclusion has established the unrivalled hegemony of English over Indian minds. This has morphed the communication pattern altogether. Literature in non-English languages is looked-down and trivialized where as sparkling wit of the short-lived variety is made much of, because of its English*ness*. This has given rise to the exclusion of non-English speaking populace which runs into tens of millions. This large mass of people then is excluded from the inner echelons of the pseudo-cultural elites.

At the same time this phenomenon gives rise to de-inclusion as well. The rise of noveau–elites. The newly English-initiated take great pride in alienating themselves from the English-illiteratti. Thus creating a different class of themselves which is excluded from the "real" cultural-elites and is de-included from their supposed social inferiors. This goes on and creates more and more such pockets of communities which are in suspended animation on account of the de-inclusion.

The loss is of Communication. The de-inclusion prevents articulate communication amongst the communities and allows for air pockets and vacuums.

These empty spaces are then filled by hi-end technology driven means of information dissemination. This takes various forms and once again is successful in creating more such islands of alienation. The process is quite simple, yet subtle and off course unintentional. Here the target is women and up-worldly mobile youth. The medium used is glitzy and kitschy films and televised soap-operas. So far as social messaging goes, it is always negative, iso-chronically supplanting all the moorings of a sound cultural base. These electronic communications drive out the archaic notions of culture and rituals and replace them with super-archaic concepts only packaged differently. The package or the expression is glossy, smooth, sparkling and vacuous. It has created another pocket of stay-at home-women, young girls and teen-agers who are "different" from their "social inferiors", who else! One more for de-inclusion.

Language and media which should be working for inclusion and away from exclusion, actually help perpetuate the schisms that help create exclusion. The difference is that, there are now differing subsets of excluded, included or de-included people.

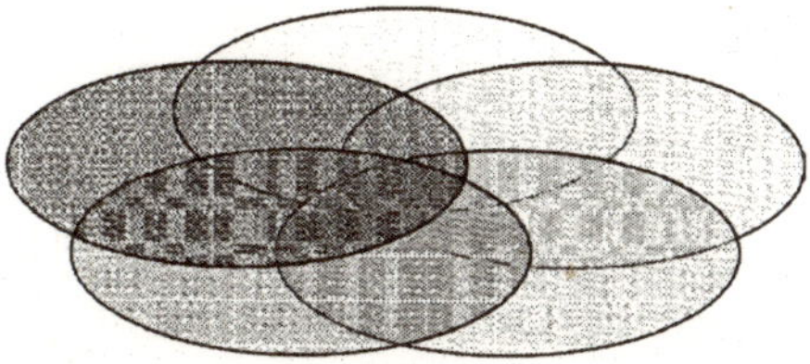

Now the society looks very much like a mass of intersected circles, which have a bevy of subgroups.

Each circle is a separate subset which also is a part of some other groups. In actual reality, it is much more complex than the diagram attempts to depict. As a result, the communication which ideally should have been a smooth flow of linear waves becomes a mass of entangled waves, criss-crossing, intersecting and bisecting. Conversations are conducted at multitudinal planes and is never a linear function of concise thoughts. The cultural ethos of the society has been subjected to diametrically differing changes, while trying to retain the vestiges of an bygone era. The loss here is of culture, conversation and communication. The reason being communication. It is like a vicious circle or the proverbial pigeons coming home to roost-kind–of-scenario.

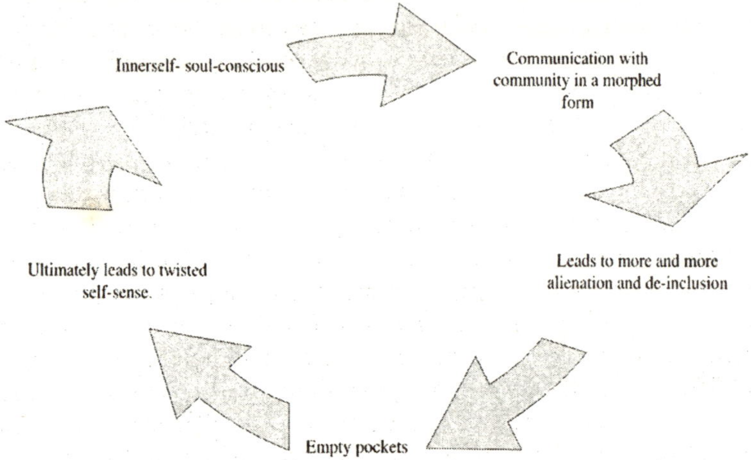

What began as a charming process of soul-searching and finding one-self is degraded into a blasé themalogy of smug sophistication. Here one is totally out of tune with everything. There is utter, absolute and complete loss of one's consciousness, ethos, identity, moorings, roots, anchor, self-sense et all... in fact all that personifies one-self. The process began with communication and ended with communication. Spiritual communication with inner beings is the starting point. However once the silent noise is smothered then the debauched degradation from ethereal innerself to a blasé outerself is easily achieved by various stages of exclusion and de-inclusion. It is an omnipresent phenomenon of everlasting nature. When one culture supplants or sometimes super-imposes another may it by language or other such means, new communities which are actually subsets of earlier ones are formed. They sometimes take on a fresh ethos which becomes a new culture.

The silent noise is the prompting which if unheeded leaves one unhinged.

Here one is tempted to quote William Butler Yeats' famous poem, "the Second Coming".

"The falcon cannot hear the falconer;
Things fall apart; the center cannot hold;
The ceremony of innocence is drowned;"

This beautiful work very aptly expresses the inner conflict with the soul and the outer confusion leading to exclusion of communities. Admittedly Yeats could have envisioned some other interpretations; however in this communicative chaos this is most fitting. It is always the silent noise within which are the promptings of the soul which are effective when in conversation with oneself and outside world. Effective communication is about identity, ethos, exclusion, consciousness and inclusion. Communities and cultures are built round it or destroyed due to lack of it.

As Yeats aptly remarked

"The best lack all conviction, while the worst
Are full of passionate intensity.
Surely some revelation is at hand;
Surely the Second Coming is at hand."
(Second Coming, W. B. Yeats)

Is the order of today? One never knows. Communication leads, guides and shows the path. Be it new societies or cultures, or civilizations built round fresh linguistic dimensions it is always the conversation which is the first step. It is born out of conflict of thoughts later translated into symphony of ideas once again expressed in conversations. This is the circle of light or vacuum which keeps turning and churning. And the circle carries on.

Once again our own din,
Of us and them
It is the world of sounds all silent
All still and hushed /
Muted whisperings on calm waters...
The Silent Noise reigns.
(Anuradha Malshe, 2008)

REFERENCES

(National Joint Committee for the Communicative Needs of Persons with Severe Disabilities, 1992, p. 2) http://*www.unm.edu/~devalenz/handouts/defcomm.html.*

(http://education.newarchaeology.com/definition_communication.php).

(http://uter.kambala.nsw.edu.au/cate_begbie/index.html.

http://www.relationship-with-self.com/definitionofcommunication.html).

http://www.businessdictionary.com/definition/communication.html.

Section–IV

Law and Governance

11

GOVERNANCE AND COMMUNICATION IN INTERNATIONAL RELATIONS– A GERMAN PERSPECTIVE

Felix Hofmann, Germany

| A person who has had an experience is the one who narrates the story well. |

Rwandan saying

CHANGING FACES

Governance in the Stone Age? If governance means communication, then yes! Governance has many faces, but they all have one thing in common: they are the mirror of our cohabitation. A million years ago, cavemen bossed around cavewomen to pick the right berries. In Ancient Rome, a society with restricted participation possibilities, public speeches were the centre of the political life. Two-thousand years later, people risked their lives to express their political opinion by the secret distribution of critical pamphlets during the Nazi regime in Germany. Today, we have arrived in the Age of Communication and governance looks different all over again. Now, our idea of governance revolves around concepts of responsiveness, capability, and accountability, focusing on communication between governments, civil society actors, as well as transnational and international actors.

Of course, the styles of communication used by our caveman were a bit more rudimental than the ones we assumed today. But when he brought himself to the leader of his little cave family, he could not have done so without communicating his intentions. Public opinion as the basis of political authority implies a key role for communication. Governance and communication are inseparable. They can be tools of conflict as much as they can be tools of peaceful relationships.[1] Governance and communication are omnipresent. They are not a result of the possibilities of our century, but came into existence as of the first cell division. They only change their faces from time to time.

THE POSSIBILITIES OF OUR AGE

The modernisation process of governance and communication is not only a peculiarity of today's media environment. In Germany, it already gained a special dynamic in the second half of the 19th century due to the impact of the French Revolution and the Industrial Revolution in England.

However, it should take a while, almost half a century, until the March Revolution of 1848 and with it a new political way of thinking opened the German society for modern political communication.

With the advent of mass printing presses in the mid-1850s and the first appearance of mass media, the German society transformed into a modern communication society. The spread of literacy and the emergence of newspapers finally replaced the world of oral tradition and interpersonal communication. The German historian Thomas Nipperdey calls this new world "a world of free choice, self-education, reflection of behaviour, change and progress," in short: a world of unleashed curiosity.

This little historical review is important in consideration of the rapid changes in today's communication methods. Today, in the heyday of blogs, instant messaging, podcasts and voice over IP, the communication of our society can be characterised by a secularisation and rationalisation of normative bases, the increase of personal mobility in geographical and social terms, as well as a pluralisation of lifestyles. We finally arrived in the Era of Communication. We have as many opportunities as never before to express our political opinions and to obtain the necessary information in order to be able to form the latter. Do we use them?

BETTER COMMUNICATION = BETTER GOVERNANCE

Globalisation has changed the face of communication. Communication adapted to world-wide decision-making processes and is therefore associated with a new form of governance. The latter now comprises the entire interaction framework of formal and informal institutions, relations, mechanisms and processes between states, citizens, markets, as well as governmental and nongovernmental organisations. In this context, actors bargain for their interests, negotiate, settle disputes, and determine their rights and obligations.

Our world is more dependent on communication than ever while at the same time communication must be effective in order to ensure the prevalence of global governance. According to John W. Burton, former Director of the Centre for the Analysis of Conflict at University College London, by effective communication is meant the deliberate conveying and accurate receipt and interpretation of what was intended to be conveyed, and the full employment of information as received and stored in the allocation of values, interests and goals.[2]

If communication is inefficient, it leads to misinformation or no information at all. In our age, we cannot afford any ineffective communication. Globalisation has brought with it a multitude of difficult and pressing tasks for our civilisation, such as inter-cultural and inter-faith relations, global terrorism, and international migration. If we want to best respond to these issues and take the most out of the possibilities of globalisation and the technical revolution, then the key lies in a global governance based on effective communication.

GOVERNANCE AND COMMUNICATION WITHIN THE FRAMEWORK OF THE UNITED NATIONS

Multiculturalism, migration, and globalisation among others are the key factors of a political, economic, and cultural development that makes an international focusing indispensable for modern democratic societies. Germany, together with 191 other nations, is a member state of the United Nations, the organisation that stands like no other for international co-operation. Established after the end of World War II, the UN is not only the most prominent international organisation of all time, but also the principal actor in international relations, which is why governance strategies and communication are crucial for the role the United Nations plays.

The UN primarily is a forum for communication between the governments of its member states. The results of the their communication processes within the United Nations are-with exception of those of the UN Security Council-not binding in international law. Much more, states *promise* to implement the agreements adopted in UN resolutions in national legislation or at least to *reflect* on their implementation. Is thus the principle of effective communication already in question?

The substantial forwarding of resolution content, political conventions, and recommendations into national policies and legislations of UN member states is one of the main starting points for criticism of the United Nations system. Too often, negotiation results at the international level, due to their non-binding nature, are not transformed into national legislation. The structure of the United Nations, being a conglomerate of the world's national executives itself, cannot provide the international system of state and civil society actors with a single executive power that is able to guarantee the implementation of UN resolutions. In this context, particularly non-governmental organisations (NGOs) play a central role in global governance.

Since the end of the 20th century, non-governmental organisations have been established policy actors which by high media presence have exerted sustainable influence on global governance. Through large-scale campaigns, NGOs are worldwide politically active and able to shape national government policies through interest aggregation and articulation. With some spectacular campaigns, NGOs won over important media representatives and increased the political impact of their own activities. Meanwhile, communication of many NGOs can be characterised by a targeted advocacy for specific topics and an effective lobbying.

The organisational structure of classical NGOs can be divided into national, regional and local branches. They do not include employees in the role of government representatives and finance themselves as non-profit organisations mainly from membership fees and donations. As thus professional, independent, societal agenda setters, NGOs have a capacious potential to ensure the effectiveness of the UN system without the presence of an international executive organ. They are in an unparalleled position to exert pressure on governmental decision-makers for the implementation of policy concerns at the national level and for a progressive change at the international level.

GOVERNMENT ACCOUNTABILITY

Communication in global governance is a means of creating mechanisms to broaden public access to information and empowering non-governmental organisations to achieve a more participatory process of policy implementation. In the below virtuous circle of transparency, 3 the World Bank

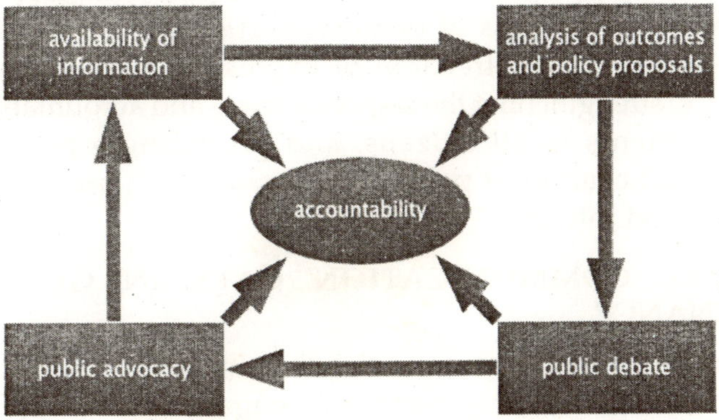

demonstrates the flows of effective communication of a governance conception focusing on government accountability.

The model originally refers to the elements of national systems of checks and balances. Transferred onto the international level, the availability of information reveals communication processes and policy decisions of the United Nations, facilitating evaluation and monitoring of outcomes and proposals through non-governmental organisations. With more NGO activism, the level of public debate rises, creating awareness of the population. As a result, international policies become more contestable and NGOs can effectively advocate their courses of action and ensure government accountability. Finally, communication generates further demands for more reliable information, increasing responsiveness of governments to non-governmental organisations.

Therefore, effective communication plays a crucial role in fostering a governance conception that distinguishes itself through responsiveness, capability, and accountability of all its actors. Effective communication improves the ability of NGOs to articulate their needs and to measure the performances of governments. It increases government responsiveness by providing NGOs with the necessary information to understand their rights in order to hold governments to account-a vital function of global governance.

In the words of Amartya Sen, Indian economist and winner of the Sveriges Riksbank Prize in Economic Sciences in Memory of Alfred Nobel, "unfettered [sources of information are] essential in the process of democratisation by contributing towards the rights of freedom of expression, thought, and conscience, strengthening the responsiveness and accountability of governments to all citizens, and providing a pluralist platform and channel of political expression for a multiplicity of groups and interests."

CRITICAL COMMUNICATION GAPS IN GLOBAL GOVERNANCE

The development of communication technologies over the past decades strengthened growth and engagement of NGOs enormously. With the proliferation of access to the Internet and e-mail communication, the possibilities for a boundless exchange of information have been advanced in a way unimaginable in the past. The technical innovations of our time enabled the international integration of global governance actors and thus a transnationalisation of non-governmental organisations.

NGOs are dependent on the effectiveness of their own communication and a transnational problem focusing. But they are also reliant on access to information essential for their respective fields of actions. In their capacity to effectively hold governments to account for policies and their outcomes, NGOs need information to make informed choices and open channels of communications operating in two directions: from the United Nations to NGOs, and from NGOs to national governments.

Since the 1990s, globalisation has become a buzzword for socio-political and economic change and has not only made an impact on the non-governmental sector. Even the far-reaching communication processes of the United Nations through globalisation are subject to change in political, economic, and cultural terms. The fundamental changes in the international system make it increasingly difficult for NGOs to comprehensively understand all aspects of communication within the United Nations.

Efforts have been made by the United Nations to break down barriers in international communication. The UN has consistently upheld the principle of freedom of information as stipulated in the Universal Declaration of Human Rights of 1948 and has organised debates, conferences, and reports on the subject. In 1960, the Commission on Human Rights decided to review developments affecting freedom of information as a regular item on its agenda. Thereafter, the Economic and Social Council (ECOSOC) requested the Secretary General to provide the UN with an annual report showing developments in communication media. The ECOSOC also called upon the UN Department of Public Information (UNDPI) to associate NGOs with effective information programmes on the work of the United Nations. In 1968, official relationships between non-governmental organisations and the UNDPI were established.

However, there is one essential aspect which communication efforts of official UN broadcasting and publishing programmes have not been covering so far and which hinders a vast number of UN resolutions and conventions to be implemented by UN member states, and this is the availability of tangible information about the commitments states make on the UN level.

CAN'T SEE THE WOOD FOR THE TREES

Regardless what field of action a non-governmental organisation has, one of the greatest problems they have to face is to be able to overlook the overwhelming amount and inter-linkage of resolutions, agreements, and related documents issued by the UN and its Specialised Agencies. Of course, the United Nations conducts several online bibliographic services and certain UN entities provide public information, but there is no institution analysing all UN conventions and resolutions, leaving the practical approach of getting a clear idea on how resolutions developed over the years, how they are inter-linked to each other, and most importantly which specific clauses in them are relevant for the work of an NGO, with unsatisfactory attention paid to in the current UN information system.

Inspired by the idea to help non-governmental organisations gain access to information about UN agreements-specific enough to enable them to use these details for lobbying purposes and effective communication-, an initiative named Making Commitments Matter (MCM) was founded in January 2008. In co-operation with the United Nations Association of Germany, a group of highly motivated university students, graduates, and PhD students from the United Nations Youth Association of Germany were convinced that by making information readily available to NGOs they could make an enormous contribution to the national implementation of UN conventions and resolutions.

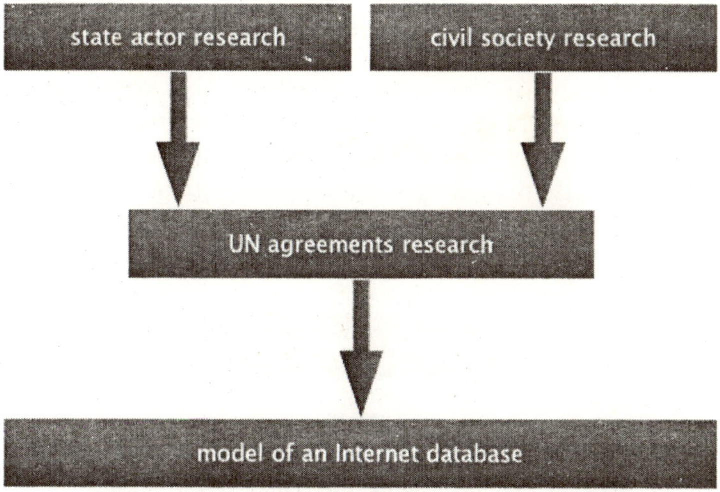

The MCM Initiative conducts several fields of research in order to reach the key players in the UN commitments implementation process. Due to the fact the individuals responsible for the implementation are certainly experts in their area of work, but the vast majority of them are laypersons in the field of UN agreements, the *UN Agreements Research* aims at developing ways of presenting the vast amount of decisions passed by various decision-making bodies of the United Nations each year in a way systematically analysing and categorising the development of specific operative clauses of UN resolutions, their inter-linkage, and their relevance for either specific fields of action of non-governmental organisations or being a normative basis upon which formal laws can be created.

Focusing on quantitative surveys among NGOs in Australia, Croatia, Denmark, Germany, Norway, Tanzania, and the USA as well as conducting qualitative interviews with NGO representatives in the eighteen target countries of the initiative, the aim of the *Civil Society Research* is to specify what enables or prevents civil society actors in taking a proactive role in ensuring the implementation of UN resolutions and what exact type of information is necessary for achieving this goal.

With its *State Actor Research*, the initiative seeks to determine information flows within executive systems in order to investigate how information about UN agreements is transferred from the nations' permanent missions to the United Nations down to the desk officers of different national ministries. Simultaneously, researchers investigate legislative processes leading to the implementation of UN resolutions in the form of formal laws.

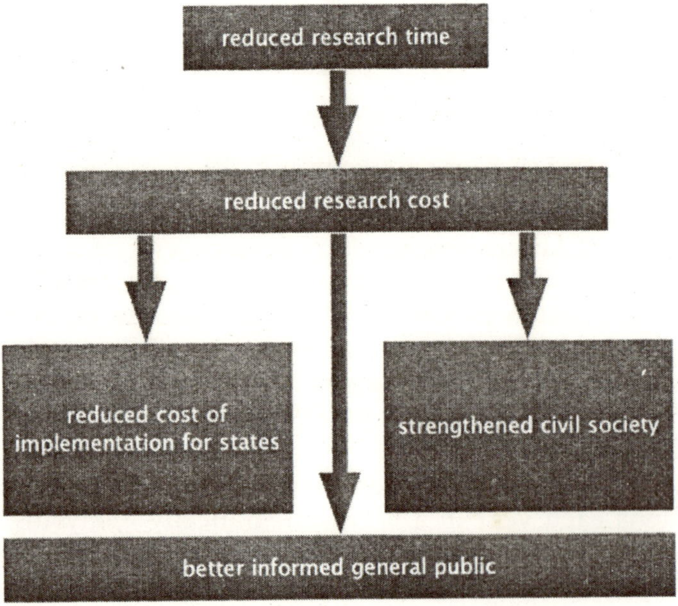

As of today, Making Commitment Matter has grown to an international initiative with more than one-hundred university students and young professionals coming from twenty countries on four continents. The MCM Initiative is aiming for the creation of a model of an Internet database which provides information on UN agreements tailored to the needs of state and civil society actors, both being equally in need of tangible information. The MCM concept not only reduces the time needed for research done by NGOs, state administrations, diplomats, and parliamentarians, lowering the costs for the large-scale implementation of UN agreements, but ultimately strengthens the role of the United Nations as a whole.

FACES IN THE FUTURE

A future-oriented governance is marked by international communication processes addressing all newly emerging areas of possible recipients. On one hand, conventional communication channels such as television and print media are to be maintained as to not reduce their existing space of impact. On the other, communication of the future must illuminate the possibilities our time provides us with, the Internet in particular.

Never has there been another way to communicate as accessible, as democratic, and as making the world grow together as the Internet. We must be careful not to let the Internet become an ocean where there is a risk to drown in information. Instead, the rapid development of technology requires us to always create the tools appropriate to help us comprehend the amount of information that rises with every second.

Still, there is a yawning gap between the communication and implementation of governance. It is the challenge of all the actors on the stage of global governance to close the gap through the technological revolution of the 21st century. Our caveman would probably use the Internet, too.

NOTES

1. John W. Burton. *Conflict & Communication-The Use of Controlled Communication in International Relations*
2. *Ibid.*
3. World Bank. *Global Monitoring Report 2006.*

REFERENCES

Amartya Sen (1999), *Development as Freedom.* Oxford University Press. Oxford.

Burton, John W. (1969), *Conflict & Communication-The Use of Controlled Communication in International Relations.* Macmillan and Co. Ltd. London.

Davison, Phillips W. (1965), *International Political Communication*. Council on Foreign Relations. Frederick A. Praeger Publishers. New York.

Frantz, Christiane (2007), *NGOs als transnationale Interessenvertreter und Agenda Setter* in: Jarren, Otfried/Lachenmeier, Dominik/ Steiner, Adrian (ed.). Entgrenzte Demokratie? Herausforderungen für die politische Interessenvermittlung. Nomos Verlagsgesellschaft. Baden-Baden.

Kiefer, Markus (1999), *Politische Kommunikation in Deutschland-Krisensymptome und mögliche Gegenstrategien* in: Haberl, Othmar Nikola/Korenke, Tobias (ed.). Politische Deutungskulturen. Nomos Verlagsgesellschaft. Baden-Baden.

Making Commitments Matter Initiative. *www.makingcommitments matter.org*

Overseas Development Institute. *Governance, Development and Aid Effectiveness: A Quick Guide to Complex Relationships*. http:// *www.odi.org.uk/publications/briefing-papers/2006/ governance-development-aid-effectiveness.pdf*

Sarcinelli, Ulrich. (2005), *Politische Kommunikation in Deutschland-Zur Politikvermittlung im Demokratischen System*. VS Verlag für Sozialwissenschaften. Wiesbaden.

Thakur, Ramesh/Weiss, Thomas G. *The UN and Global Governance: An Unfinished Journey*. *www.unhistory.org/ publications/ globalgov.html*

World Bank, *Development Communication Division. http:// siteresources.worldbank.org/extdevcommeng/resources/ devcommwhatwedo.pdf*

World Bank. *Global Monitoring Report 2006. http://siteresources. worldbank.org/intglobalmonitoring2006/resources/2186625-1145565069381/GMR06complete.pdf*

12

LAW AND COMMUNICATION-TOPICAL CHALLENGES CONCERNING EU-AND EC-LAW

Martin Weber, Belgium

CAN EUROPE LEARN FROM SENECA?

"Laws ought to be short (in order to be understood more easily)"[1] -Even today, scarely anybody would dare to dissent from this claim Seneca set up almost two-thousand years ago-at least not at first sight. With "understanding being nothing else than conception caused by speech"[2] -as Thomas Hobbes has put it-it seems that a canonical, general rule can be phrased stating that the more words as elements of speech frame a law, the more difficulties arise in comprehending the latter due to the increased number of possible errors in the conceptional process. Obviously, exceptions have to be acknowledged: Nobody has the ability to decode a cryptically truncated legal rule resulting from an adbridging of a long, but precise sencence just because of the fact that it is short. In addition, Seneca's statement describes only one dimension of the intelligibility of law disregarding a lot of other factors influencing its perceivability. Some-like language and diction-are rooted in the law itself, whereas others find their bases in the addressees. These may be the single intellect of the individual as well as personalized interpretations of legal rules.

Intense academic research has been carried out for centuries to define the parameters of comprehensibility and their interdependencies and for finding ways to ameliorate the understanding of law.

But why is law deemed to be understood? Seneca himself just latently scetches perspicuity as an underlying aim of all law as do most scholars today, but does not name the matter for this. Today, broad consensus prevails about the fact that law is inter alia a means of communication between an authority (mostly the state) and its subordinates (in the majoritiy of cases the citizens) or two parties operating on equal terms. Every party in a bi- or multilateral relationship created by law is equipped with certain rights and/or duties, whose existence and exact content is conveyed (=communicated) to them by the law. As a matter of fact, communication can only prosper with all participants being proficient in applying the medium which is law. The basis therefor has to be understanding. For Seneca and many academics this was apparent and clear so it remained unspoken.

Currently, Seneca's general benchmark for measuring the quaility of laws in terms of understanding has been deemed an ordeal by the hypertrophy of laws resulting from the European integration process. While most legal provisions as such range in an eligible length, it is the exploding and unmanagable number of legal norms composing European law as such which probably make Seneca turn himself over in his grave. The first and central question which is to answer in the following hence will be if this enormous amount of legislation actually aggravates the "legal communication". After that, other problems related to the aformentioned factors especially considering language and interpretation will be examined.

SELECTED PROBLEMS OF LEGAL COMMUNICATION IN THE FIELD OF EUROPEAN LAW

Needlessly to say, only the most important and crucial points of issues concerning quality, style and language of European law important in the communication context can be depicted here. To faciliate the understanding for readers not having any juridical knowledge, to whom this text actually is aimed at, no deep-going detailed law-related remarks are included. Most problems discussed are of general and global interest; the European Law merely acts as a makeshift to exemplify them.

From the Initial Founding Treaties of the European Communities Until Today-An Overview

1. The initial Treaties setting up the European Communities: With the process of European integration rapidly gathering monumentum after the Second World War, intergovernmental and supranational institutions and organisations were set up on an international level to achieve close cooperation between the participating states. Besides the Council of Europe[3], three European Communities were installed by the Treaties of Rome and Paris in the 1950s. The most important Treaty signed was the Treaty establishing the European Economic Community (EEC), which is in force until today though being renamed in 1992. It contains inter alia a bundle of substantive legal provisions mainly conjunct with the economic field. As the Community creates a new legal order, rights and duties under the Treaty are not only conferred to the contracting parties (i.e. the states), but also to the citizens of the member states. These substantial Treaty provisions are fully valid law which can be enforced in the national courts of the member states. As a consequence, everybody doing transboundary business in the communities had to be informed about the advantages EC-Law grants and also eminently about the risks and legal forbiddances it contains.

Especially since the internet as source of insight and information did not exist, a multitude of citizens were halted and confused about the legal situation. Brochures and informations fairs were scarely offered by the authorities so only few people investigating on their own account could gain a vague insight what the new European Law was about. This lack of communication was put into perspective taking into account the fact that more often than not only companies with legal departments or individuals having been counseled by lawyers beforehand participated in the international trade. As so often lawyers inhered and still inhere a bridge-building-function between the nomothetic body and the addressee. They do not only act as legal advisers, but rather as interpreters conciliating between the two parties. Unfortunately, most clients completely rely on the skills of their lawyers and do not even try to acquire themselves some knowledge about the law. Communication in legal concerns therefore always is contingent on the advocat as auiliary person except in very basic cases. The working of the legal system would be much more efficient if people would abandon their stereotypes about law being an inscrutable mystery and develop some sense of justice preventing them from getting into legal difficulties. Many lawsuits and disputes could be avoided if individuals would inform themselves about denouements in law in general lines from time to time by reading newspapers or asking authorities to send them materials which are in the majority of cases for free. If lawyers would act not only as sole interpreters, but as cooperative teachers, they could ignite the client's will to learn about the law - some kind of "language" he uses in everyday communication. Some lawyers are of course reluctant to share their precious knowledge with the client, for if the latter discovers that legal counseling is superfluously, the lawyer will not be hired again. With some lawyers even being suggestive of the law being a miracle, emancipation of the citizens in legal matters will remain a pious hope.

2. *The flood of secondary legislation:* Most EC-Law is not codified in the Treaty (primary law). The latter provides institutions and mechanisms for enacting legislation, e.g. in the form of directives or regulations (secondary legislation). With amendments of the E(E)C-Treaty, the Community was given legislative competences on various, not only economical sectors. That development went along with an enormous amount of secondary legislation bothering several areas of life. Especially since the Single European Act expanded the Communitiy's competences, even lawyers face difficulties in keeping pace with the frantic germination of secondary legislation fueled by the Treaties of Maastricht, Amsterdam and Nice.

In addition to that, directives which generally have to be implemented by the member states to become operative sometimes are directly effective meaning that citizens can rely on them in national courts without the directive being transmuted into national law. This is only possible if the directive fulfills certain requirements and only in a vertical dimension (relationship citizen–authority). If no direct effect can be granted to a directive, it still can inhere indirect effect, denoting that the national provision has to be interpreted "in the light" of the directive by the national courts. This thoroughgoing simplification of the system may just give a cue about the intrigacy of the system.

With the extension of the Communitiy's competences and in an age of globalization, virtually every citizen of a member state potentially has to apply European Law in his everyday or business life. Due to the complexity the legal system has developed, problems can most hardly be prevented by informing oneself beforehand, for law has become most fugacious, protean and intricate, so that even specialized lawyers face difficulties in classifying and applying the appropriate rules. A massive hitch in communication now arouse, for even the "interpreters" are unable to understand the "language" they should translate in. Even the authorities, who have created the law as a means of communication, fail in knowing it in its entity. The consequence is a minatory communication breakdown in the long run in combination with the stagnation or a collapse of the legal system. So Seneca was right regarding the fact that too big an amount of laws entails incomprehension with the consequence that the communication system identical with the legal system perishes. The enormous compounds of law presuppose a exponential growing complexity of references in the legal structure and a non-managable accumulation of legal norms hardly anyone can cope with.

3. The case-law produced by the European Court of Justice (ECJ): In addition to the written statutory sources of law, there is tremendous bulk of decisions by the ECJ.

The latter elaborated a bundle of so-called "general principles" underlying the whole Community Law and having been employed by applying a legal instruction. Generally, this is a positive thing for everybody can forebode how a Janus-faced legal provision is interpreted and has to be adopted. Nevertheless, normal citizens the law is targeted at fail more often than not to identify this unwritten criteria oblique in thousands of pages of difficult juridical decisions. Plausibly, nobody could yearn for everybody being bound to buy a textbook on EC-Law and study the chapters related to the general principles by hard for this is too sophisticated a thing–sometimes even for studied lawyers. What could be done to ease understanding for EC-Law would be to make a list of the general principles, explain them in few, graspable words and hand them out to the citizens of the member states. But instead, most effort was made in promoting the European Community by printing book- and leaflets alluding to topical EC-problems or achievements of various nature without explaining the underlying political and juridical background in some simple words. Sometimes, some information material provided by the EC-institutions may even be misinterpreted by the citizens: A sample for that are little books containing the Charter of Fundamental Rights of the European Union provided by some delegates to the European Parliament being suggestive of this Charter being operative by employing phrases à la "Your Rights". An evaluation of this material being a main channel for the communication of law to the citizen is therefor of utmost importance and urgence. The same claim applies to the internet pages of the EC-institutions. In order to fullfill the claim some lawyers expressed, a high level of transparency should be reached by making all legal documents accessible. The outcome of this well-intentioned undertaking is a complete mess of documents being of interest only for lawyers, not for the citizens. Notably the pages of the ECJ contain only few materials the normal citizen is capable to understand, most of which only tells him about the composition of the court and the building it is placed and thus is rather nugatory. Even after having inspected the internet pages by heart, people without any legal knowledge will barely be able to evaluate to what extent EC-Law affects them. Ocularly, a lot of money has been spend in the homepages and information material of the European Community, but unfortunately it is most beneficial for those who already have legal knowledge and want to deepen it. Again, it is the citizen ignorant of the legal system and needy of legal aid who is left behind.

A second aspect of the EC-caselaw not only baffling normal citizens, but also lawyers and national authoritys is the interpretation of the substantial provisions of EC-law. By this, sometimes methods are consulted rooted not principles common in the legal systems of all member states. From time to time, it is extremely demanding for the parties to apprehend that the EC has created a system different from the national one in many respects. Some fail to accept the differences, get embittered and refuse to accept the legitimacy of the EC-law. For the communication process this exhibits a complete breakdown as one of the parties refuses to cooperate and participate in it.

The most important third aspect of case-law ist that as a source of law, the more judgements there are, the more confusion about what the legal core of a norm and therefore the binding interpretation is arise, especially with many judgements being extremely contradictory. Again, this development contributes to the lack of understanding due to the explosion of the legal sources.

4. *Additional Protocols added to the Treaties:* As some states opted out of some Treaty provisions and especially secondary legislation, protocols had to be annexed describing the exceptions being made. At the one hand, this raises difficulties for the citizens in descrying the applicableness of a rule in their country, on the other hand it creates the feeling of inequitable treatment among them. There are only few cases where citizens are directly affected by deviant rules, for more often than not only political hassles are solved by it. Nonetheless, this protocols contribute to the inpenetrability of EC-law and cause disaffirmation among the citizens for they seem unfair. Moreover, they contribute to the humongous aggrandizement of EC-Law making it uncomprehensable.

5. Conclusion: Summing up, there are a lot of lacks in communication between the EC as legislator and the citizens (and states) as addresses.

Especially for the understanding and acceptance of law among the citizens, the EC has to simplify law by reducing the number of legal sources which ought to be indexed properly. The law has to be promoted and spread by comprehensible materials provided by the institutions as well as inteligibly designed web pages. A continuing revolution based on consecutive evaluation is indispensable. The EC–respectively–the EU has a long way to go.

Special Problems Related to Law as Part, Content and Means of Communication

To enhance EC-law and law in general, one has not only to pay attention to pass an adequate amount of law in the legislation process, but bear in mind also factors accountable for their quality. Below, examplarily problems related to law as a language of its own and to interpretation of the law discussed.

1. Law as a separate language: As the EC-Law applies to the legal relationships of citizens of the member states conversing in various different languages, one frankly might assume that this implicates lashings of conflicts. In reality, however, EC-law can be translated adequatly and fitting into all the distinct languages in nearly every case, so that conflicts clash only sporadically due to obscure interpretation. The multiple misapprehensions occuring by virtue of the fact that not all the EC-staff (judges, civil servants) is fluent in the working languages of the EC which are English and French is a different kettle of fish. The latter is some kind of phenomenon cropping up every time people sharing not the same language having to cooperate. Even the Bible refers to that in the story about the Tower of Babel. This is no failure of the law, but more of the people using it. A solution for this issue has not been found yet, but its negative impact can be reduced by educating people and nurturing them being cosmopolitans. Learning foreign languages is in this context of exceedingly importance, as is the knowledge of foreign cultures for developing a sense for cases a litteral translation is not appropriate and target-orientated. Emendation is of course always possible, but the EU and EC have undergone various gainful endeavours minimizing conflicts.

What is more relevant than the challenge of law being transmuted in different language is law forming a language of its own. In the legal language, many terms used in everyday life have a different, shortened or extended meaning. Difficulties arise especially with words being used as synonyms in normal language. In some contries, the translated equivalents of "possession" and "property" may be utilized to describe the same, namely than a specific item is attributed to a specific person. In some legal systems however, "possession" marks the factual and actual power over the item, whereas "property" refers to the legal correlation of the item to a person. As a consequence, an individual can possess an object which is in its property at the same time. The tenant of a flat possesses "his" domicile, whilst conincidentally the dwelling remains in the property of the landlord A thief possesses the purse he has just stolen, though he is not the proprietor. If this possession is just is another factor one has to examine. This very basic example most people are aware of points out the hair-splitting logomachy prevailing in law. As EC-law has to use terms in an uniform sense at the international field, it may occur that some legal terms have the adverse meaning at the EC-level as at the national level in some countries, for most other countries use the term in a sense which is compatible with EC-law. The consequences of this of course are wonderment, incomprehension and refusal among the citizens of the concerned member state.

As an additional aspect, neologisms are created in the area of law often by combining two or more commonly known words giving them a completely different meaning one might suppose. Sometimes even latinisms are employed to give law a special august touch and turning it inscrutinable for everybody not having savoured a humanistic education. Serendipitously, at least the latter over-sophistication of law was not employed in EC-law.

What also is a riddle wrapped up in an enigma to most citizens is that the syntax of a legal norm can indicate which party is imposed the burden of proofing facts. A negative phrasing of elements within a legal norm can be a hint to the burden of proof being turned vice versa. Of course, this principle of reversing the duty of presenting evidence was employed only in the official translations of the legislative EC-acts in languages of member states whose lawyers are used to this gimmick. Nevertheless, for the normal citizen this prudent trick is hardly to grasp.

With law being an artificial language, communication and understanding concerning non-legally trained citizens is considerably hampered. The underlying area of conflict with the claim of law being clearly understandable for its addressees on the one hand and the need of clearly defined terms to work with on the other hand has to be solved in a balanced compromise developing a more comprehensive and citizen-friendly law. In this respect, a lot of work has to be done.

2. *Law and its interpretation:* "Let all the laws be clear, uniform and precise. To interpret laws is almost always like corrupt them" Voltaire wrote 1764 in his Philosophical Dictionary. As law has to be both concise and sharp-cut for being applicabe at the one hand and exerciseable for a multitude of similar cases on the other one, there are different possibilities to what extent interpretation is employed. If one acclaims the dictum of Voltaire, for each very special case one can imagine a law has to be written so that no interpretation is necessary. The antagonistic way would be to employ one legal norm for all cases which of course needs interpretation to fit for every situation. Voltaire's way is definitely not the best, for it produces a multitude of norms nobody is able to understand, and therefore conflicts with Seneca's view. So is the other way superior? As a matter of fact, norms would have to be phrased very general and vague to be adaptive for every situation. Gaps and breaks would have to be filled by interpretation, but by whom? Of course a judge or a lawyer can stress what his or her subjective impression on the intentional meaning of a provision is. With both of them being

not democratically elected, the citizen might develop the speculation that his fate is in the hands of the abitrariness of a third person corrupted and spoiled by personal emotions. Both lawyers and judges would be given legislative power though not conveying their force democratically of the citizens and furthermore ignoring the principle of the separation of powers in terms of judges. Law would become a nebulous, unpredictable case-by-case-system dependent of the discretion of each judge. Uniformity, clearness and preciseness, the goals that Voltaire lined out would be elided. A reasonable solution therefor only can be a compromise between the two reverse perspecitives: Generally, Voltaire's notion has to be converted for the sake of justice with employing vague provisions requiring to be interpreted only to evite an explosion of legal sources and the accomplished collapse of the system caused by a lack of comprehension by the participants. Here, the EC would definitely do better do allow more interpretation inuring to the benefit of clear and short legal provisions.

CAN EUROPE ALSO LEARN FROM VOLTAIRE?

As it has been shown, Seneca's dictum about coherence in understanding and lengh of a legal norm is generally true and EC-officials would do good with taking Seneca's remark to their hearts as they seem to have done in relation with Voltaire's bonmot.

But in his "Philosophical Dictionary", Voltaire also articulated another claim: "Voulez-vous avoir de bonnes lois; brûlez les vôtres, et faites-en de nouvelles" (If you want good laws, burn those you have and make new ones). Most people definitely would share the view that this call is too irrational in its radicalness. Nevertheless it includes a lot of truth in its core: If law becomes an abiding peeve, drastic reforms are necessary to create acceptance for the revised law among the citizens for if the addressees do not obey to it, law looses its right to exist. For the sake of justice far-reaching reforms have to be tackled to develop the muddleheaded mess EC-law is at the moment into the gainful and marvellous system it was intended to be.

FURTHER READING

To get a general idea of EC- and EU law, there are a lot of excellent textbooks available. Some of the most recommended may be

- *Craig, Paul / De Búrca, Gráinne :* EU Law. Text, Cases and Materials, 4th edition, Oxford 2008
- *Lenaerts, Koen / Van Nuffel, Piet:* Constitutional Law of the European Union, 2nd edition, London 2005.

For informations about the difficulties in understanding EC-Law, reference is made to http://*www.clearest.co.uk/files/ClarifyingEC RegulationsCont.pdf*

Finally, it might be useful go get some general idea about the problems of legal language, style and interpretation. A lot of books have been published dealing with this topic, a few of which are

- *Garner, Bryan A.:* The Elements of Legal Style, 2nd edition, Oxford. 2002.
- *Lerch, Kent D. (ed.):* Recht verstehen. Verständlichkeit, Missverständlichkeit und Unverständlichkeit von Recht, Berlin/New York, 2004.
- *Marmor, Andrei*: The Pragmatics of legal language, USC Legal Studies Research Paper No. 08-11, http://*papers.ssrn.com/sol3/Delivery.cfm/SSRN_ ID1130863_code49181.pdf?abstractid=1130863*
- *Mellinkoff, David*: The language of the law, Eugene 2004.
- *Patterson, Dennis*: Interpretation in Law, http://*www.trinitinture.com/documents/patterson.pdf*

NOTES

1. Seneca, Epistulae 94.38 ("leges breve esse opportet (quo facilius teneantur)").
2. Thomas Hobbes, Leviathan, Part I, Chapter IV.
3. The Council of Europe is not an EC- or EU-institution. Therefore no further reference is made to it.

Section–V

Business and Communication

13

MAKING PRESENTATIONS: GETTING THROUGH THE FIRST STEPS

Mohandas Nair, India

INTRODUCTION

Making good presentation is a major aspiration, at least for the guys in corporate jobs. The fact is that when you make presentations you are noticed. And when you are noticed, you have a chance to grow. However, making presentations is not for the faint hearted, and getting through the first stage is the difference between success and failure.

According to Sir George Jessel:

"The human brain starts working the moment you are born and never stops until you stand up to speak in public."

Sir Jessel is making a very important point here. Going blank when we are up in front of an expectant group for people can be the most embarrassing moment for an individual. Even if we manage to start off, our audience will be focused only on our discomfort, disregarding what we are communicating at that moment. Our purpose is thus not served. Besides disappointing the audience we also disappoint ourselves and probably feel ashamed of ourselves. We could avoid speaking in public in future.

BEING NERVOUS

Being nervous is part and parcel of making presentations. The degree of nervousness is the issue. Very high degree may lead to panic attack, which blanks our thought processes. We have failed badly in our communication effort.

However, a low degree of nervousness is not only OK but also essential to the presentation process. It indicates a desire to do well. It gets us to prepare well for the presentation. The nervous energy can be canalized to deliver a presentation with better impact.

An individual, who has no nervousness and full of confidence, could be on the brink or over the brink of overconfidence. This inducement into a false sense of preparedness could get the presenter to under prepare and to deliver a less that good presentation. Sometimes an aura of superiority could cloud the performance leading to alienation from the audience.

Thus, handling the nervous energy is the first task of the presenter.

This nervous energy experienced is a result of the fight/ flight response, which a person experiences when threatened. Making presentations are always perceived as threatening. This is because you take center stage and is the focus of a group of people who have expectations from you. You do not want to belie their expectations and also want to form a good opinion about yourself among them.

Having a particular personality trait can provide some benefits. For example, an extroverted personality (someone who is very comfortable dealing with people) normally is not affected much by nervousness when called upon to make a presentation. The fight/flight response among such people is muted and they have a certain level of confidence in delivering their message. However such people are prone to over confidence, leading to inadequate preparation and hence a not too effective presentation.

SHARING EXPERIENCE

For an extremely introverted individual, it was indeed a stressful journey for me, a decade and half ago, to achieve today's level of comfort and confidence in making presentations. More effort was needed to facilitate programmes through getting the participants to share their feelings and experiences and bring out the learning from such discussions. This shaping of my personality to be comfortable in a public speaking process has enabled me to change my perception of a group being threatening to be comfortable in them.

I had to fake my mind into thinking that I was an extroverted person and that I was indeed very confident about being able to stand up in public and deliver. This I managed to do through continuous visits to the "hot spot" and looking directly at the many pairs of eyes looking askance at me. Over the years I used various strategies to continuously tune my mind on this issue and, today I can say that I am fairly good at making presentations. I rarely break into a sweat and can hold on to the "here and now" situation for up to a five day program.

To improve my confidence I have used various strategies over the years and continue to do so. I have read some books for tips, but no reading has helped me become a better presenter. I had to be up in front of that audience and deliver.

I would like to share some of my processes, which have helped me to build confidence in making presentations; at least to make a good start:

(1) I accept invitation only to present topics of interest to me. I must be excited about the topic. I should want to research it and get as much information as possible about it. I should be able to demonstrate a passion for the topic when delivering it. If I do not have the passion for it, why should others be interested in it? My passion for the topic and confidence that I can handle it, and answer relevant questions, helps me to build up my confidence for the delivery.

(2) I want to be able to get to the root of the definition of the topic so that I can build my program around it. This will help me to have a strategy to introduce the session, to make a start. Knowing how and where to start is an issue of concern for most speakers. This will

set the tone for the program. The participants also gauge a program on how it was introduced and decide on whether to focus on the program or drift away into something else. A clear understanding of how to make a beginning helps a lot to calm nerves.

(3) I would like to know who my potential participants are. Are they senior, junior or middle level participants? A mixture would be a terrifying prospect, unless it is only to do with facilitating. I can tune my mind to structure the program accordingly and also work on appropriate examples, stories. At a very senior level program I facilitated for a very large organization, in mentoring, a couple of participants informed that they would not participate in any role-playing exercises!! Building confidence at a feeling of being in control helps calm nerves.

(4) I spend adequate time in structuring the program based on the feedback from the client. I insist on having a through discussion with the client on their program objectives and expectations. This will help me to fine tune the program structure and organize for relevant tools required for conducting the program. I make sure that the whole program is designed well in advance and a copy of the structure provided to the client. I also ensure that the study material and tools for duplicating are available with the client in time for their use. This takes out some pressure from me.

(5) A day before a major program I will not want to have anything to do with it. I keep myself occupied with other things and avoid thinking about the program.

(6) I am always at the venue an hour before the program. When the program is out station I arrive the previous night. Good rest before the program is necessary.

(7) At the venue, I check on the seating arrangements. I always prefer a discussion group arrangement as I build in a lot of participation. Most of the time the

arrangement is not what you want and it takes some time to rearrange. Sometimes you may have to even change the venue. Doing this at the last moment easily produces nerves. I walk around the venue, sitting in some participant chairs trying to get their perspective. I soak in the feel and try to make the venue seem familiar.

(8) I check all the equipment, check for the location of the switches, walk around the venue looking for the location of the washroom, any discussion rooms, tea break and lunch break stalls, etc. I get introduced to the venue coordinator and any other person who would be of help. Take down any phone numbers, which could be used in an emergency.

(9) I load my matter in the computer, check for smooth flow of material and also if the matter could be seen well in the last row. Also which switches to be switched off to brighten the screen. I check the collar mike and test its audibility around the room. I also arrange the documents for discussion in a sequence as per the program structure.

(10) I take a few deep breaths and do some bending exercises for good measure. Then a final check-up at the washroom before going back to receive the participants.

(11) When the participants enter I greet them cheerfully. This is not my natural style, but I have learned to do and am comfortable doing it now. Shaking hands helps to build a psychological bridge of friendliness. I also get a gut feel of how many participants are unsure about the program from their grip and think about what I will need to do to ramp up the interest in it.

(12) After the introduction of the faculty I take a final deep breath and am ready to start. I introduce myself in my own style and since I have done it so often, I am comfortable doing it. Slowly my passion takes over and I am on my way!!

CONCLUSION

Getting off to a good comfortable start is the basic requirement in making excellent presentations. Since first impressions are lasting it is important to make in good. The rest of the program will follow suit.

Mohandas Nair is a management educator, a teacher, trainer, writer and a facilitator of learning. He earned a B.Tech (Mech.) from IIT Kharagpur, India, has a diploma in training and development, and has thirty plus years of experience in industry and consultancy in the fields of Industrial Engineering and Human Resources Development. He has published two books, written numerous articles and facilitated management development programs.

14

COMMUNICATION AT WORK PLACE

Mala Mody, India

Marriage is said to be like a delicate thread... The same can be attributed for "Communication at Work Place" A small misunderstanding can blow the association like a house of cards...!

God has beautifully differentiated every human being from another in every aspect; for e.g. Phsyical Appearance, Actions, Thoughts, and most importantly, the way every person interprets similar situtions at different times. When a child cries, the mother thinks he is hungry, the father might think he is not well, and the grandparents might think something else altogether.

Similarly at any work place, employees at the top level have a different way of thinking and interpreting conversation or situations; when compared to the employees at the middle and the lower level. Inorder to have a condusive work environment, it is really important to bring together these thought processes; and the only way which can make this possible is "Effective Communication".

Communication is the process of attempting to convey information from a sender to a receiver with the use of a medium. Communication requires that all parties have an area of communicative commonality.

It is defined as a process by which we assign and convey meaning in an attempt to create shared understanding. This process requires a vast repertoire of skills in intrapersonal and interpersonal processing, listening, observing, speaking, questioning, analyzing, and evaluating.

> *Communication at Work Place means the way company personnel communicate with each other can make all the difference between efficiency and ineptitude, success and failure, making money or losing it*
>
> *By Azriel Winnett*

A work place can have two Formats:

(1) *Formal Work Place:* Formal organization is a fixed set of rules of intra-organization procedures and structures. As such, it is usually set out in writing, with a language of rules that ostensibly leave little discretion for interpretation. Practical experience shows no organization is ever completely rule-bound: instead, all real organizations represent some mix of formal and informal. For e.g: Reliance, Tata, etc.

(2) *Informal Work Place:* At an informal work place, there are no set rules and regulations. Decisions are taken/ moulded according to the situation. Communiation is required to be informal inorder to create a comfort level for the employee. The examples for the same are:

(a) House maids/Servants.

(b) Event management companies.

(c) Watchmans.

(d) Roadside Vendors etc.

It is important for service organisations/people engaged in providing services that involve the customers for the final delivery of the product, to make the customer feel comfortable with them. It is ver important to empathize with the customers. The provider should try making the customer feel safe with him; and all this is possible only if the provider is able to communicate informally with the customer. The level of informality should not be so high that it leads to infringement of privacy for the customer.

In this way, Communication is important for both formats inorder to inform and engage people at work. The different approaches for communication available are:

(1) Written communication

(2) Verbal communication

(3) Grapevine

Communication can take any of the forms mentioned in the diagram given below.

(1) Written

(2) Verbal

(3) Grapevine

(They will be discussed later).

(4) *Signs & Symbols:* very commonly used while packaging. It acts as a common language across varied countries.

(5) Eyes: very often it is said that emotions can be observed in the eyes of the sender. For e.g. it is said that when two persons are in love, it can be seen in their eyes.

(6) *Noise:* is often used by children to show their feelings. For e.g. a child starts crying when he wants something but doesn't gets it.

The most popular forms of communication used at work place are Verbal and Written.

These two forms can further be divided into Formal and Informal. Written communication which takes place through E-mails, Letters, Memos, etc are considered to be more formal and as compared to verbal communication. Companies, now days prefer communicating through E-mails, as they are not only eco-friendly, but it can also act as a legal document.

As far as verbal communiation is concerned, the most widely used language all across is English. This is a language which helps integrate all cultures, religions, & Castes. This is the language which is often used in a conversation between a boss and an employee, between a new joinee and his collegues and in meetings. Once the new joinee gets used to the office and his collegues, i.e. when he is in his comfort zone, the language automatically change from English to either Hindi (Indians) or they start communicating in their mother tongue. Communicating in mother tongue makes people more comfortable while sharing their problems or their happiness. In India where the quality of spoken English is not that goo and that, many people still do not know English, conversing in his respective mother tongue makes the person at ease.

The third widely known form of communication is Grapevine. Normally verbal communication is used to develop a grapevine, but with the growing popularity of this form, I have differentiated it as a separate for of communication.

Grapevine (gossip), is a term often used to describe a form of informal communication, as in "heard it through the grapevine"

It is often known to be "The Unofficial path of verbal communication". Rumors or scuttlebutt are spread from person to person through an informal network. Traditionally Grapevine is often cinsidered to be a bad form of communication by any organisation. But, with the changing time, organisations (The Management) realised that they can use this method in their favour to check the reaction of their employees for a particular decision/action that they may or may not execute.

But, Grapevine Comunication always has more ill effects rather than having positives. Information gets distorted in a grapevine communication, and this can be detrimental not only to an individual or a group of individuals but also, the organisation as a whole.

Having transparancy in communication at work place is vital for not only running the organisation smoothly, but also to retain employees-who have become the most important assets for any organisation.

The above can also be categorised as ways of Free Communication. But, like every coin has two sides, even free communication has certain obstacles. In a nut shell these are:

(1) *Fear:* Fear is an emotional response to threats and danger. It is a basic survival mechanism occurring in response to a specific stimulus, such as pain or the threat of pain. Psychologists John B. Watson and Paul Ekman have suggested that fear is one of a small set of innate emotions. This set also includes joy, sadness, and anger.

One of the core reasons for ineffective communication can be attributed to "Fear".

Fear can be of anything. For e.g:

- In an interview, the candidate is gets nervous, the reason behind this can be, fear of not getting the job, fear of not being able to impress the interviewer.
- If one fears of losing the job because of the efficiencies of his collegue, then he spreads rumours.
- Most importantly, human beings fear other Human beings, be it the subordinate, the superior, wife, children etc. this is a major reason why communications turn out to be ineffective.

This fear creates insecurity, which ultimately leads to loss of confidence in a person. With this lost confidence, communication turns out to be ineffective.

Insecurity for an individual can be in Objective sense or it can be Psychological i.e. emotional insecurity.

At any work place, out of the many emotions they are present, the most widely known, but hidden emotion is Insecurity. Insecurity at work place can be categorised into the following:

- Insecurity of losing the Job.
- Insecurity from collegues.
- Insecurity of being less competitve.
- Insecurity of getting less compensation.

Feeling inferior to others in the organisation etc.

These feelings often influence the way a person interprets the message in conversation thereby leading to miscommunication.

(2) *Trust: Trust* is a relationship of reliance. Trust is a *prediction* of reliance on an action, based on what a party knows about the other party. Trust is a statement about what is otherwise unknown—for example, because it is far away, cannot be verified, or is in the future.

Let us consider a real life situation to understand the implications of Trust on Effective Communication.

(Names Changed)

ABC organization wanted to recruit a person at the managerial level for the position of Corporate Relations. There were two Senior Executives (Rahul and Prashant) within the organization itself who expected that they will be promoted, as the HOD had promised them. But finally a new person (Naina) was recruited from the industry. Naina was young and beautiful, but at the same time she was dynamic. As far as Rahul & Prashant were concerned, the HOD promoted them to the position of Assistant Managers. The HOD thought that everyone in the department was happy. But the real situation was something else.

Rahul, who was naina's junior became friendly with her. As Naina was new to the organization, because of this gesture she too started feeling comfortable with him. Slowly, Naina started sharing her observations in the organization with

Rahul. She started sharing almost all her emotions related to her boss and colleagues with Rahul. Rahul took advantage of this situation and started Gossiping about the other employees in the department with her; which resulted in Naina believing and creating an impression of people around her on the basis of what she heard from this one person Rahul, who she had just met. And she started behaving in a different manner with her other subordinates, and also her boss. Finally one day when Naina confronted the things said by Rahul, with Prashant, she realized that Rahul was simply using her to remove his grudge of not being promoted to the position for which Naina was hired. And this led to Naina realizing her mistake of relying too much on a person and began to change her attitude towards her work mates.

(3) *No trust:* Means not showing any reliance on people around i.e. Lack of trust in collegues

The reason why lack of trust is considered as the basis for unproductive communication can be seen in the paragraphs coming ahead.

"Lack of trust" is one of the most important grounds resulting in ineffective communication.

Often when a person enters the corporate world, or so called the corporate jungle, he/she is warned by everyone around him to be cautious of others. He/She is given all sorts of negative feedback like, people are not good, they can never think well about him/her, he/she can never make friends there as everyone there works for their own selfish motive etc.

Even I was said the same thing. So I developed a shield or a boundary around myself, and never allowed any one at the office to cross that. I always considered good gestures of people as negative; I never interacted much with colleagues and behaved like a thorough professional. No doubt, this behavior had spread the news through the Grapevine Communication that I was a "Khadus" and made my subordinates very uncomfortable whenever they had to share any problem. This created a gap, and I was not considered to be approachable, which was absolutely not a sign of my subordinates being happy with me. And this was proved by a fall in their productivity which directly resulted in declined profit.

In short, I joined the office with a negative feeling about people which ultimately made me behave/communicate in a manner which I initially was scared of.

When one doesn't trust his collegues, then even if someone tries to do something good for him, he refutes to believe/ show faith in the other person. He/She feels that the information has been distorted for personal benefit and starts interpreting the basic idea of the information given; according to what he thinks is appropriate.

Some more parameters which help identify the level of trust are:

- The person's basic nature
- His/Her attitude
- His/Her believes
- His/Her upbringing
- The situation in which he/she entered the conversation.
- And the most important, his/her convenience.

The objective behind taking these two extreme cases of trusting people and not trusting people especially for a communication topic was to demonstrate that; if one is scared of someone, then he cannot strike a good conversation with a person; and this fright can be reduced by creating a level of trust in people around you. It completely depends on you how much you trust the other person.

Also, many times the level of emotion (like Loneliness, Sadness, Fear, etc.) around us is so high, that we lose control and let our heart rule our head resulting in spoiling relations with many people; just like Naina in my example. If you try to take control of these situations, and try striking a balance between a your professional and personal life; even 20% of times; your overall communication at work place would be healthy as compared to what it is right now.

To sum up, Effective communication can be related to making Good Food. Good food is the outcome of mixing the right ingredients i.e. the vegetables, the spices, the intesity of fire etc. by the Chef.

Similarly, inorder to effectively communicate a message, the sender, just like a good chef, sholud try to maintain a balance between the spices i.e. his internal emotions like fear, insecurity, trust etc; the vegetables i.e. the external environment which includes the collegues, compensation etc; and the intensity of fire i.e. the words spoken or heard; so that the message is interpreted in the most effective way.

REFERENCES

Communication-http:*//en.wikipedia.org/wiki/Communication*

http:*//www.hodu.com/business-communication.shtml*

Diagram- Mala Mody, 2008

Written communication-*http://en.wikipedia.org/wiki/Communication*

Verbal communication-*http://en.wikipedia.org/wiki/Communication*

Grapevine- *http://www.answers.com/topic/grapevine-1*

Fear- *http://en.wikipedia.org/wiki/Fear*

Insecurity- *http://en.wikipedia.org/wiki/Insecurity*

Trust- http:*//en.wikipedia.org/wiki/trust*

15

STRAIGHT TALK

Mohandas Nairs, India

INTRODUCTION

Credibility is a virtue worth reaching out for. You are trusted. You are liked. You say what you mean and mean what you say. You are always in demand. You will always be wanted. You are one step ahead of everyone, just because you are believed.

The underlying thrust of credibility is "straight talk". Speaking clearly, directly and honestly without rudeness or humiliation to the other person or group. In straight talk you tell them as it is. There is no strategy to mix up the communication to make it hard, soft, ugly, smooth, whatever. You firmly believe in what you say and are ready to be questioned on what you say. You may be wrong in your assumptions because you may never have all the data or information to provide the perfect response; but you honestly communicate what you believe in. If found to be wrong, you are ready to change your viewpoint and do it with humility.

According to Kaleel Jaimson, the foundation for straight talk includes the following:

- Respecting others enough to be honest with them
- Passing information in a way that produces an efficient, effective environment for communication

- Developing individuals, and
- Utilizing differences

WHEN YOU STRAIGHT TALK

When you straight talk, you are honestly communicating your perception of what you think and feel about the situation. The situation may be something else according to another, but what you communicated is your perception based on your knowledge and experiences. This will provide sufficient ground to make a start in whatever we choose to proceed to. There are excellent chances that we are on the right track. The other person who respects you for your straight talk can make a straightforward choice to decide on the situation and move on. There is no waste of time to rethink the issue and in the need to look for some more options. We may never get the right solution for a situation in life; however this situation could be the best to decide on and proceed.

WHEN YOU DO NOT STRAIGHT TALK

When you do not straight talk there is a deliberate attempt to distort the communication. The receiver of the communication, initially, may trust you, but in the future, on being unable to succeed as expected due to your faulty communication, will reject your communications. You will not be credible to him/her. If the loss to the person is a major one because of your faulty communication, you could be assured that you may lose credibility in the eyes of a few others too. If the others are important to you, you will be starting with them on the wrong foot.

STRAIGHT TALK CLIMATE AT THE WORK PLACE:

Organizations, which profess and create a climate for straight talk, are bubbling with enthusiasm. They save a lot of energy and cost in their operations. For a start there will be very little duplication in communication. There will be no memos sent after a phone call to ensure that the recipient does not deny the communication. There will be no need to cross check data or information as the communicator, valuing his/her credibility, ensures that the information provided is true. There will be no repeat calls from customers, suppliers and others, as they will respect your message that you will keep them informed about issues as they crop up. You will not want to let them down. You will contact them as needed so that they can formulate an action plan for themselves and avoid unnecessary delays. Even if you cannot deliver as promised, they will appreciate your frankness and believe in whatever you communicate.

MANAGING MISTAKES/PROBLEMS

A major problem is with mistakes being "swept under the carpet" as you do not want to be penalized for it. The bump under the carpet could trip others and when they lift the carpet to revel the hidden issues, you could be penalized for hiding it in the first place. Either way you could not escape. The reality is that nothing can be managed without mistakes. Everything we do is based on assumptions and they could be wrong. The best strategy would, thus be, to come clean on the mistake and face the music early. The issue could be solved quickly before it festers and grows to a size calling for drastic measures. Better to act quickly. Better to talk straight on the issues confronting you.

MANAGING OVER DISTANCES

Managers who have to manage people and processes over large distances have to create a climate of openness in his/her group if they have to manage effectively. For the manager operating from Mumbai, whatever is happening in Vietnam is a mystery. He/she will know only what the representatives in Vietnam choose to reveal. Unless the true situation is addressed, decisions will not be right and effective. Getting such personnel to talk straight will provide the manager relevant inputs to take proper decisions to move the processes in the right direction.

PLAYING POLITICS

Politics, of the negative variety prevents efficient and effective functioning of the organization processes. Individuals do not know what to do in certain situations. They hesitate to take action, as they are not sure where they stand in the situation. They do not want to be hurt. The decisions and action they take may not be appropriate or unnecessarily delayed. This will adversely affect the organizational processes. A climate of straight talk will go a long way in reducing the politics in the organizational processes, enabling better and clearer understanding of what is to be done or not done.

FEEDBACK

Feedback is a process where our behaviour is relayed back to us, by another through their perceptions of what happened when we acted. We get to know how the other received our behaviour and if it was in line with what we had intended to do. Feedback allows us to introspect on our behaviour and plan ahead to continue to behave in the same way or modify our behaviour in future. We can understand why we were a success or otherwise. We can make corrections in the way we behave in future: learn something new, do something different, or anything other to enable better results.

When feedback is perceived as straight talk, we do not have to check on their validity and reliability. We can just take it and work on it. We are confident of obtaining positive results.

MAKING PRESENTATIONS

Persons wanting to communicate to a large group of people make presentation. It could be about selling a product, policy, service, and an idea. If the person is not seen to be credible the entire process will be a waste of time and other resources. The audience needs to buy-in to the communication and this they will do only if they feel that the presenter is giving the matter to them straight. The presenter can only do this if he/she understands the topic of presentation, and all the issues connected with the topic. Since nothing is perfect in whatever we do and use, the credibility of the presenter will be enhanced when the presenter also talks about the negatives of the topic-what should be done to ensure that the negative aspects do not interfere with the processes being talked about. The presenter's gestures and tone of voice easily communicates his/her intent. Any attempt to mislead will be understood easily, the audience will tune off.

USING "I" STATEMENTS

When you use "I" statements, you take responsibility for your actions. You affirm who you are and what you want. Obviously you do not want to project anything other that positives about you. You want to be seen as a credible person.

"I" statements are powerful because they are factual, and as an observation on your part, they are non-negotiable. They describe the world as you see it and the way it affects you directly. You are describing the interpretation of a situation, not just the situation itself. It tells the other person directly the effect their behaviour is having on you.

When you connect them with your feelings, they are powerful and non-negotiable or irrefutable. No one can challenge you and say that you don't feel that way. The statement lets the other person know your exact position and what you expect. They don't have to guess. They can only say "Yes", "No" or negotiate. The other person neither knows what will happen and so there will be no surprises.

MANAGING CONFLICT

When two people come together, the ground is fertile for conflict. Each person being different has different viewpoints on issues and so there are chances to disagree on issues. Straight talk implies bringing the matter to the awareness of the group, matter as each individual sees it. Once the group in conflict knows what individual perceptions are they can work to change the perceptions as needed or at least negotiate matters so that there is some resolution to take the matter forward. As Kaleel Jamison states: "The skills involve listening to yourself and the other person, clarifying what the other person is saying, then staying with your own point of view and with the conflict in a respectable way that says you regard your partner as a worthy interactor".

CONCLUSION

Being known as a person who talks straight will make you credible in the eyes of the other person. You will not need to justify your assumptions. You can sell your programs without making significant efforts. You will get the backing and support of others in your endeavour. You will have a better chance to succeed.

REFERENCE

Kaleel Jamison (1985), *The OD Practitioner,* Vol. 17, No. 2.

16

UNFORGETTABLE LESSONS IN COMMUNICATION

Vikram Nabar, India

INTRODUCTION

The word "communication" evokes a vast spectrum of languages and written words; new technology and equipment out on the market; variety of educational courses in the field of soft skills, personality development, mass media technology; and people being expected to "make a difference" by acquiring skills in the use of new equipment, etc.

Communication consists of conveying information and emotions. This is not restricted only to humans. Some of the other life-forms (amphibians, reptiles, birds) are thought to have their own sounds of communication. Mammals (especially apes and monkeys) are very expressive. Dogs are known to pro-actively do a disappearing act when a punishment for naughty behaviour is being discussed.

Within human society, as social organization has become more sophisticated, effective communication has become increasingly important. The cave-people inscribed messages and pictures on stones and cave walls, and this practice continued through many centuries. Inventions in paper and printing technology (Gutenberg Bible was the first–known mass production in printing, using blocks) brought about a revolution and a sea change in the written communication scenario. Until then, scribes had been writing everything by hand in ink, which was the original. If a copy was needed, they would write the whole matter again.

Communication through touch, paralanguage, body language, spoken language, has been in existence since time immemorial. While one can only guess at the forms of communication in earlier times, it is clear that in a modern economy the methods have evolved from face-to-face dialogue and argumentation to written letters and hard copy instruction manuals, which then gave way to emails and soft electronic copies. As the dependence on impressive software and hardware to support communication has grown, the toolkit of "black-box" computational procedures has expanded rapidly. The electronic toolkit is now being relied upon to perform computational tasks that even a few decades ago most engineering students would have been expected to reason out from first principles using the underlying calculus and algebra which is now pre-coded into the "black box" procedures available in scientific software packages. This can have a negative effect on productivity unless the adoption of the new technologies is accompanied by an emphasis on maintaining effective communication and cooperative, non-hierarchical approaches to problem-solving. Contrasting examples of good and bad communication strategies illustrate the importance of this point.

BENEFITS OF GOOD COMMUNICATION

On a freezing cold morning in February 1995, as a part of a business seminar for Indian Managers held in Tokyo, we had visited the NEC Corporation located close to Mount Fuji. Their Managers had welcomed us, after which their PR person went on to explain:

- "Speedy and correct *Communication* is the key to optimize human potential.
- Over the past years, the changes anticipated in Business Environment and the growing significance of *Computerization* are in focus everywhere

- In tune with this, our mission has been set as *C& C for Human Potential*...we innovate and sell products & services, against global competition, to satisfy the needs of our clients"*

Thus had begun our factory visit. Later that evening in my hotel room, I pondered philosophically over the wonderful day gone by. One part of my mind said, "Communication is successful if and when the sender sends his message tuned to the capability (frequency) of the receiver. The objective is to get across, the information and the emotion as accurately as possible."** Another part of my mind asked, "Isn't that a rather simplistic interpretation of what I saw today? At an advanced level, I have been boggled by seeing the innovative products that are serving humanity's needs of communication. But at the fundamental level, I have also experienced first hand, NEC's demonstration (communication) of their mission statement in action. It has been a 100% satisfying experience from macro to micro, enhancing my knowledge throughout the visit".

The experience at NEC reminded me of a meeting in February 1983 at my workplace in an MNC. All the managers were being given a pep-talk on the impending winds of change, by an enthusiastic Danish Managing Director who had been posted in India on a three year stint, "My dear friends, your success as managers will largely depend on how you communicate with your fellow-workers, peers and superiors. Our company will soon be installing an advanced computer system. One needs to be even more precise when one is communicating with a computer, because a computer will never be a substitute to human thinking. Always remember the GIGO principle, *"Garbage Input leads to Garbage Output"*.

---

* Only a summary extract of his presentation is quoted here. *No other Company's mission statement has ever stuck in my mind as much, as that of NEC.*

** One will find the analogy in Radio-tuning. But, since the receiver radio has to be tuned to the frequency of the transmitter, the analogy is in a "reverse" form.

This was exactly the same early childhood lesson I was fortunate to have received from my parents, "Incorrect communication results in wastages".

FALLOUT FROM POOR COMMUNICATION

Together with the positive memories of the visit to NEC, some opposite situations have also been etched in my memory. I apologize at the outset, should a mention of them (necessary in the context of some aspects discussed later) be hurtful to any reader(s). Over the last 15 years, to keep up with the changes in the business environment and to enhance their organizations' efficiency by providing adequate enablers of speedy communication, the top management of most Indian organizations made heavy investments in sophisticated equipment (macro-level peaks). Their intentions were good. But in some cases, the investments appear to have been effected without analysis, or without ensuring that the employees were trained with the requisite knowledge of the micro-level foundations (basic business systems).

Take the example of a company who were leaders in Capital Goods product lines. Their standard products were made in batches. But a large percentage of their business also served customers who were ordering one-off non-standard products for projects. At one stage, they abruptly invested in an advanced Manufacturing Resource Planning (MRP) system, most effective in mass production. Having done that, the logical path should have been to tread cautiously, by restricting the system's introductory use to batch-production of proven products. Instead, they started using the system for products/components on one-off projects, and also for parts of prototypes at design and development stage. The ensuing confusion hit the company's operations badly. These self-created problems had not even been understood (let alone analyzed and sorted out), when somebody sold them the idea of cost-savings by using a Business Process Re-engineering (BPR) software package. This made the situation even worse.

The Detrimental Effect on Productivity had Resulted from Large Gaps in Internal Communications

THE LOST FOCUS

The importance of effective communication is only likely to grow in the future, as the tasks become even more specialized within a knowledge economy. An indicator of whether our future workforce can meet this challenge is their current state of understanding and communication of topics covered in their courses.

From my experience of teaching engineering and management subjects, I would like to alert the readers to the alarmingly decreasing desire and initiative amongst a growing percentage of students to

(i) go into the depths of a subject,

(ii) be able to dig out facts,

(iii) be able to communicate adequately and appropriately.

A culture of doing things in haste has also been evolving simultaneously. In support of all above statements, I would advise my readers to see the exam answer-books in relation to the questions asked. If the exam results are bad, the students blame poor instruction from the teachers, while the teachers counter the charge by accusing the students of not studying. Some of these very students go up the corporate ladders, and at some stage start to follow their followers (*Aladdins* becoming servants to their *genies*).

For day-to-day miscommunication at higher levels, we do not need to search deeply. As an example, look at the modalities of how the Indo-U.S. nuclear deal was executed by our national leadership. Lack of openness/pro-active communication with all other political parties led to speculation, heated tempers, and fodder for newspapers in the form of accusations and counter-accusations. The result as usual: wasted resources from the point of the common man.

One can't be far from truth, if one says that (i), (ii), (iii) above need to be cultivated in early childhood. Steps need to be taken to encourage curiosity, and to create "questioning" minds amongst the students from early childhood schooling.

To summarize from these examples, in previous decades when workers received less help from sophisticated equipment (even simple calculators were rare), they paid more attention to basics. But as the 20th century progressed and technology evolved, making innovative equipment and software packages (enablers of speedier communication) more widely available, the workforce has started to take a lot of things for granted, and has been giving less and less attention to learn the basics of communication etiquette. *The missing link, communication etiquette, has become progressively weaker and weaker, and needs to be restored/ strengthened.*

RECOMMENDATIONS TO MAKE COMMUNICATION MORE EFFECTIVE

Often I have been asked, "What are the etiquettes (the whats and the hows) of successful communication? Can you please elaborate on the habits of successful communicators? What type of training in communication is required during the formative years of a person? What facts need to be pro-actively communicated at an individual or organizational level, to avoid the damage control later?"

The above questions do need to be addressed as critically as possible, but there are no straightforward answers. From my experience, some do's (etiquettes) listed below go a long way at improving communication and the overall work efficiency. The list is not exhaustive. One can add to these items, as one goes along.

Communication is not Just Sending out Messages It also Involves

- Asking the (5W, 1H questions, viz., what, why, when, where, who and how) and finding out the required information. A mere Top-Down approach of class instruction will need to be replaced consciously by bringing in a healthy culture of interaction/asking questions in order to challenge the assumptions made. This habit needs to be inculcated early in life

- Looking back (reflecting) upon comments/statements, and getting to understand from the speaker (sender of the message) importance of what he exactly meant
- Recording and circulating the summary of decisions. For instance, after an office committee meeting, the Chairman should arrange to circulate these details, which serve to facilitate a forward movement (prevent repetition of earlier discussions) when the committee meets the next time
- If a team is stuck for direction, the team-leader with his experience, must give alternate proposals for action, after which the team discusses and zeroes down on the path to be taken. The leader thus communicates and controls the team to keep it on track. A team consensus has a high degree of success when compared to a Top-Down approach of a military order.

Etiquettes at an Individual Level

- Identify the target audience for whom one wishes to send out a message. Find out as much as possible about their interests. For example, if preparing to address college students, find out about the college's attitude towards sports/debating, etc.
- Make all efforts to bring yourself (the sender) to the level of your target audience
- Keep the message and its language as simple as possible. Stick to the time allotted. Brevity is essential.
- Use supportive facts and logic to make the communication powerful
- Relieve monotony while communicating with comfort breaks and by introducing humour.
- Present any data visually, by the use of graphs (with appropriate units for the axes as applicable), matrices, mathematical equations.

Etiquettes At an Organizational level

- Display the Vision and Mission statements, the Organization chart, Quality Policy, etc., at prominent spots throughout the Organization.

- Give the new entrants/trainees a free access to the Company Policy Manual. Arrange to induct them into the Organization's culture at the hands of experienced employees, who have the required knowledge and skills to reinforce the Organization's ethics stories.
- Educate the employees by arranging interactions with the company's customers and vendors. The employees must be educated about the importance of growth, trade cycles, market forces, competition, peak and slack times.
- Publicize the quality requirements of customers, job skills requirements and productivity expectations (performance measures) from the management, effects of bottlenecks, stoppages, cause and effect analyses, as also the incentives and rewards schemes for quality and productivity.
- Constantly communicate to the employees (relevant) global technology advances through in-house magazines. Train them as and when necessary.
- When introducing changes, reduce the resistance to changes by holding several informal meetings of all the personnel affected. Holding such meets through picnics at scenic spots away from the usual workplace is known to go a long way towards improved working.

The Author is solely responsible for the views expressed in this Article.

INDEX